ESSENCES OF TRUTH

Inspirations for Loving Life

Anne Round ē Love

ANNE ROUND

1st edition published in Canada 2020

Essenscesoftruth.com

Essencesoftruth@gmail.com

Anne Round

Essences of Truth
Inspirations for Loving Life

ISBN 978-1-7770637-0-2 (paperback)

This book is dedicated to

My husband Adrian
Our children James, Phillip, and Jessica
And to my unborn grandchildren.

Thanks for helping me love myself while loving you.

Thank you, Wren, may your wings take flight.

Table of Contents

Welcoming Words

I am writing these essays hoping to give you food for thought. I do not know when or where you were born nor do I know the circumstances of your life. I do know that everything is always changing in us, around us, and on our planet, Mother Earth. The one constant I do trust is that we are energetic beings and our foundation is love. It is from this perspective of love for myself, love for you, and love for all humanity that I bring forth these ideas around my beliefs and my lifestyle for your contemplation.

I have always had an interest in wellness. I love being active. I did yoga, meditation, sailing, skating, skiing, and soccer in my youth which cumulated in doing my degree in Physiotherapy. I continue to be an active life long learner as new interests pique my curiosity. I regularly meditate, practice Tai Chi, dance, and engage in many creative pursuits. I am passionately engaged with my outer and my inner life.

I have always been fascinated by the magic of life ever since wading around at the yacht club catching tadpoles in various stages of development. When I was pregnant with my children, I felt the absolute miracle of life developing inside me, followed by the wonder of each child growing and expanding their horizons. Then the emergence of a young adult from a teenager always developing, expanding the miracles that we all are. Every one of us has arrived where we are today through this process of continual change, ever expanding and becoming more. We are never static as our biological and energetic systems are dynamic flowing states, converting forms from one phase to another, cyclical, and never ending. We are miraculous, mind-blowing, and awe-inspiring creators.

I have come to a place of deep compassion for myself and others, each on our own journey of life. My years as a physiotherapist involved teaching people to care for themselves so they could be their best and care for others. I saw many people who always placed themselves second to everyone around them much to their own detriment. Taking care of our bodies, mind, emotions, and spirit is our responsibility and it is an inside job. No one else knows our inner workings as we do, so we are in charge of ourselves. Once we take care of ourselves throughout life, then it is easy to extend our caring to others and support them in their journey.

Loving myself created a major turning point in my journey of acceptance. It has allowed love to flow in all areas of my life with ease and grace. Our capacity to love ourselves more and more in all situations and circumstances means we can love others for being just as they are in all ways. This stance of love for ourselves and others opens the door to trust whatever is happening around us. Truly loving ourselves is a constant work in progress which deepens in a felt sense every time we say, "I love you" to ourselves or anyone. It means stepping into trust and accepting that the universe is for us in every moment.

It is our choice to live life lovingly or not. We always have the choice to see the best in ourselves, other people, and situations. This allows us to pause, evaluate, and consider before we react to situations. It means we are aware that we might not have all the information as to why someone behaves in a certain manner. Does it mean we accept any forms of abuse? Absolutely not! No one has the right to bring harm to another through words or actions. Respect is a keystone of life. Respect for ourselves and others is essential to motivating kindness, caring, and empathy in our world.

We all get to choose how we move through our interactions with other people. My choice has been to lead with kindness and respect. These may seem simple ideas yet they are not always seen in our world. The other day as we were walking a child yelled at his playmate, "You idiot." It was loud, it was jarring, and it was obviously not remotely true. Our words, our actions, and our thoughts reflect what is inside us. In the case of a child, they are likely reflecting what they have heard elsewhere, and they are trying harsh words to gauge others' reactions. We have the power to choose our words and the old adage, "If you don't have something nice to say, don't say anything at all," is worth considering.

In contemplating our words, it is vital to observe how we talk to ourselves in our head and out loud. Being loving to ourselves means being kind, generous, and gentle with ourselves. Being understanding with ourselves when negative thoughts arise about ourselves is a powerful way of loving ourselves. Switching a negative thought to compassionate words of patience, understanding, and acceptance can transform a reaction into an ally instead of it remaining in a defensive posture. Doing so with ourselves creates the lifestyle choice to then treat others with the same generosity, compassion, respect, and dignity.

These essays speak to my choices for my lifestyle and my way to be in the world. I hope that you will gain some small wisdom from my words and embrace the love that I have for you and all humankind. I know that you are a precious human being. I pray that you see yourself with love always. I will love you forever.

Essences of Truth

Part 1 - Being Alive

Being alive is our common ground: we are all human consciousness living in a body of biology that supports our time on earth. The length of our stay and the quality of our time here is variable. Our size, shape, and looks are all unique and diverse, a wonderful tapestry of different beauty being expressed. Each of us is a unique individual human and we are all the same source energy. Every one of us was born of our mother's womb, a miraculous creation of egg and sperm joining and replicating into the trillions of cells we are. Our cells work co-operatively to function as the multitude of systems in our bodies that keep us alive. Our systems run beyond our awareness, breathing for us, signalling us to eat, supporting us as we move around, repairing and restoring us as we sleep, and all that is the miracle of being alive. We are far more the same than different. We each have a desire to be love, loved, and loving. It is our basic nature to give and receive love. Every one of us arrived as a baby; pure love, innocence, and beauty. These traits are the Universal Oneness that we all are.

Since being born, our experiences have shaped our lives into what you see today. Initially, choices were made for us, beliefs were imprinted on us, and conditioning settled us into our ways. The early years infuse us with layers of ancestral beliefs and conditioned patterns. It is our choice later in life to sift through these instilled ideas and decide which we will honour and which we will reject. This is the adventure of being alive, a constant series of choices. The bottom line always being are we choosing from love and joy, or fear and stress. The choice is always ours, as free will reigns in the human experience.

May we all choose wisely as we journey forward on our path of being Oneness, alive as a human being.

Who Am I?

"We don't see things as they are, we see them as we are." Anais Nin

I once had a powerful dream in which I was in a crowd at a party. I left the party and walked through a village of Tudor style houses. The village was circular and felt like a labyrinth. I found myself at the north end of the village and I went into a house. There I was told I had to write a test to continue on. I agreed and sat down at a desk to write the test. I turned the page over and the only question that had to be answered was, "Who Am I?" I laughed and started to write, then I woke up. The question "Who Am I?" has sparked debate for eons. Philosophers have considered this question from many angles and scientists bring their perspectives. We each adopt our own beliefs as we grow and expand. Through my years of meditating, exploring, and reading these are my views.

I see each of us originating from a single Source. The Oneness that binds us all together. Every human, animal, plant, and rock are part of this origin. It is the Big Bang theory. Each of us is Oneness expressing in its unique way. A beautiful thread in the tapestry of life, ever evolving. The energy of the One is present everywhere, always in everything. It is integral. It is always present. It is the ground from which all comes forth. It has many names: Love, Divinity, The Universe, Source, or All That Is. Any name we give this phenomenon is just a label created from our singular point of perception. One term I do like is "The Mystery." This comes closest to my experience of this unknown, unnameable source from which all has been created and emanates.

I see The Mystery as a primordial soup that creates like boiling water bubbles. Some creations escape the soup and carry forward, creating upon themselves while others recede back into the soup to be returned to the whole. Once the energy has coalesced into being, it has its own trajectory. Creation creating upon itself into all we are and see around us. Everything containing the original energy of Source. All of nature: all the stars, the animals, the plants, the rocks, and us are the same energy. We are all made of stardust and mystery swirling into human form. We are born, grow, and follow our own path of meeting situations and experiences. We live our lives in whatever manner we choose and then we return to The Mystery as death arrives to complete this life cycle.

I see myself and everyone as a being of light. When we arrive in this life, we each have an energetic blueprint that carries our gifts and talents. These traits are either enhanced or hidden as we grow up in our various conditions, cultures, and times. The hope is that we align with our highest gifts during our life to bring them forth for the highest good of humanity, nature, and our planet. Beyond all the talents we carry into this life, our essence is light and love.

I know that loving myself as the miracle I am, as a divine being carrying gifts, has allowed me to open to love, acceptance, trust, and faith in life. It has made my days flow with greater ease and grace. It has expanded my friendships. It has given me the courage to accept the end of other relationships. Loving myself allows me to stand in my own truth, and walk in the world with peace, love, and joy always.

I can feel my light alive and in motion within my being and I can feel it radiate into the world. Energy is always in motion; nothing is static just like the primordial soup. Light, energy, and love are words I interchange as the movement of The Mystery in all of us. When I honour the light in myself and others life flows with more compassion, freedom, simplicity, and pleasure.

Many voices may argue that my beliefs are naïve and have no basis in science. All that may be true or not. Science and spirituality seem to be coming together in the world of quantum knowledge. For me, living my life following my intuition has brought me a feeling of deep peace and acceptance. Intuitive signals are the way energy speaks in our human system. Allowing The Mystery to influence my life has brought me unbridled joy that words cannot truly capture or convey.

I have trained myself to trust my intuition. I listen to my gut and follow its prompting. I discern what is a yes and what is a no for me. I have practiced, believed, and seen the results of entering The Mystery and allowing it to guide my life. I know myself as a piece of the greater whole and I trust that I belong. I love myself fully. I am being a perfectly imperfect human being living life with joy. I am enough, I have enough, I do enough, and I am being enough. My basic needs are more than met and I can freely dream a beautiful world for all into existence.

I send my blessings and prayers out into the world for those who struggle and suffer. I model my choices and ways of being for those who care to see. I honour all of life and the choices that each of us makes as we walk in this world. I choose to believe that life is working for us and with us, not against us. As such I am willing to cooperate with life to expand peace, love, and joy here on planet Earth, our home. Our home, heaven on Mother Earth, I love this and encourage myself to see heaven here, now, always.

I believe, that holding the beliefs I do, allows them to move more and more freely in the world. There is deep suffering in our world; I acknowledge that. I am here to be a ray of hope for those in need, to extend my energy and love outward, and to bring light into dark places. This means being a clear beacon to guide others to safe harbour. That harbour is love. I am a house for light. I am a lighthouse of love, as are you. It means helping when asked, walking gently on the earth, and trusting life is good.

May all beings know they are love.

Lineage and Legacy

"What we do now echoes in eternity." *Marcus Aurelius*

Our children, grandchildren, and the generations ahead are our reason for creating peaceful, loving, and caring lives that honour Mother Earth. When we keep a wider view open for future generations, we consider our actions now. Our children and their children will inherit the Earth in whatever manner we leave it. The importance of creating a peaceful, sustainable world is paramount. The flame of love that we carry for future generations needs to light our path now.

Through our genetics, we leave some of ourselves here on Earth; perhaps blue eyes, thick hair, or long bodies. Rapidly, as each generation births another, the tree of our ancestry expands. I have researched family history for many years. My father planted the seeds of interest when I was young and he was researching more of our family line. I can trace my grandparent's lines back in time for a few generations. It makes one realize the immense web from which we each arise. The variety of experiences, both good and bad; the personalities, known and unknown, and the lives lived in their best way possible. So much history flows through our biology. People leaving their families, their homeland and coming to unknown territory making the best of situations that would arise. The courage and fortitude of our ancestors is remarkable. They built new lives in unfamiliar places, whether they crossed oceans to new continents or travelled across countries to new homes. We are very resilient in the face of change and new situations.

We have ancestral memories inside our cells of these historic people and places. Our biological ancestors contribute to our present physical, mental, and emotional expression and experience. We contain the lineage of our mothers and our fathers in our biology and we have a third influence on our existence. That is our spiritual lineage: the journeys that our soul has travelled across time and space. Imprints of experience from past lives that are energetically within us as we venture into this life. Reincarnation and past lives are debated by many. The Christian history removed all reference to reincarnation in the 3rd century A.D. while Buddhism considers that we do return. Karma is discussed as the situations and entanglements that come forth into this life that need to be resolved on this planet as a place of action. As our world has become a smaller place through increased technological advances, travel, and rapid communication we have the opportunity to explore the multitude of beliefs that exist and their origins in ancient times. We each need to keep an open mind and allow for possibilities that stretch our conditioned beliefs and allow our own heart to decide what is our truth. I like to keep my beliefs flexible and fluid to new information and experiences.

What follows is an account of a completely different perspective that I have gained from years of shamanic journeying, meditation, and hypnosis. Truth or fiction does not matter, it has expanded my life and brought greater acceptance of me by me and this has enhanced my life and my relationships in life. I have come from the stars and I am created by stardust, as we all are. I was present when it all began, a creative energy in the cosmos ready to expand into more. I worked with a team; I still do. Our mission, as it were, is to be love and peace. I am a master of serenity; my energy can calm hearts and breed confidence, trust, and hope. I have travelled the cosmos and I still do in some multidimensional way. I entered into this universe through the stargate Aldebaran; we see a physical representation of this place is our night sky. This system is a place of divine feminine energetic leadership. I have spent much time in the Pleiades star system immersed in various activities on different stars in the system. I have worked with the human design forever. I am one of the many star beings that came to earth as the grand experiment. On my initial voyage to earth, I did not make it. I died in the incubation chambers that were required to adjust to this new place. I succeeded on my second voyage to be here as the consciousness I am. I was in a new light body that was augmented for the experience. On the voyage by starship, I looked out the window and all my heart and soul fell in love with Mother Earth. She is such wondrous beauty, my heart grew, my love for her and her people expanded. I survived my voyage and entered into the long story of this planet's history. I lived as a Lemurian for many lifetimes. I have memories of being more light than physical skin and bones. Walking was not on the ground; it was more gliding along. The crystals were in constant communication with us as guardians of the earth and honoured companions. Lemuria was a time of great love and peace; it was part of the last golden age. Alas, the descent into darkness had begun and the human became more and more a mind-centered being than a heart-centered being. This evolution spanned over tens of thousands of years as various ages came and went upon the planet. Many lifetimes, many new cloaks of density to create the illusion of not remembering who I am. Always the pulse of love and peace penetrating every lifetime if I in the human form could allow it to exist within me. As this is a dualistic dimension all sides of the game have been played, have been experienced.

Now we are at a new juncture where we are no longer descending into darkness. Instead, we are allowing the light to infuse our very physical being and turning the long history of the human story into a return to the light we once were and are. Now we know our wholeness as the dark also. We are on a voyage of returning to love. We play out this story every lifetime to remind us of the grander unfoldment that we are playing in. We arrive, a new conception full of light and love. We grow in the womb and feel our mother's experiences. We are birthed into the world through a small, constricted canal. We are conditioned into beliefs and limitations by the traditions of our families and cultures. Our truth, of being love, is restricted over and over until we do not know ourselves anymore. Somewhere, somehow, we reach a point where our destiny turns around and we begin to return towards love and being the light, we are. Whether this is a sudden event, a gradual opening, or a deathbed experience is no matter. We return to love. We are mirroring the process of the grand experiment of the universe, a micro of the macro.

This grand experiment has a vital link for success that did not exist before. We, the 144,000 lightworkers, are here on Earth as embodied humans. There are star seeds around the globe. Somehow the intentions and desires for a shift have had to come from ourselves here and now. Past experiments have failed due to the imposition of change by other star nations over humans. Now we are part of humanity and we are instigating the change we wish to see. We can transmit the codes that are needed to change from within. These changes into unity consciousness ripple out for all mankind to receive and use in their systems. It is similar to a grassroots movement where those who need the change the most implement it and allow it to expand outward. No longer relying on those above to control the desired outcome. This is what is happening now at all levels, the same micro and macro.

There is a deep feeling among people that as the energies are shifting, we need more connection. Many humans research into their past to know their biological history and equally many are taking journeys into their inner scape to know their spiritual history. Both are seeking connection to the greater unfolding of the human journey across time and space. The desire to sense and know oneness and unity is augmenting for each of us. To recognize our selves as so much more, while being a droplet in the universe is awe-inspiring. Trusting the process and path of embodiment and the return to love as a group is beautiful to observe and acknowledge.

May we all know ourselves as the love we are.

Inside our Cells

"The happiness of your life depends upon the quality of your thoughts." Marcus Aurelius

Deoxyribonucleic acid, DNA, is a molecule in a double helix structure containing sequences of amino acids that carry genetic instructions for life. As a teenager, I remember reading about the discovery of the structure of DNA, the double helix and I have continued to be fascinated through my years. In university, genetics and developmental biology added to my wonder of life and how DNA expresses. Nowadays we continue to learn much about DNA. Gratefully we seem to have moved beyond the term "junk DNA" for those parts that we do not understand. Now the term non-coded DNA seems a more appropriate word for the unidentified parts. Today we can trace lineage, origin, health factors, and other information from our DNA with an easy swipe of the mucosal membrane in the mouth. The genome project has also shown us how our genetic makeup is not much different from an earthworm. This points to many more factors being involved in the expression of DNA to create the multitudes of species, including humans, we have on this planet.

Years ago, I had the pleasure of listening to Gregg Braden[i] speaking at a conference. The piece that struck home was about DNA. Essentially, scientists had taken samples of DNA placed them in a vacuum and transported them a distance from the source person. The person was then shown scenes that induced various emotions while the DNA was monitored for any response. It responded. First, regardless of distance from the source person, the DNA reacted when the images changed to scenes that elicited a change in emotion or vibration in the person. Second, the vibration of the emotion either caused the DNA to contract and tighten or to relax and loosen. The findings showed that uplifting emotional images relaxed the DNA and fear-based images contracted the DNA. This made so much sense to me as a physiotherapist. Clients who were wound up tight as a top and spoke with fear-based attitudes did not heal efficiently. My first task with all clients was to calm their fears about an injury and give them confidence in their ability to heal and recover. This opened the door to relaxation and augmented the healing potential within their psyche and cells immediately.

I understood that their DNA was in such a state of contraction from worries and fear that their system could not begin to create the building blocks to allow healing to happen. My treatments increased blood flow, therefore, oxygen into the areas of injury. This allowed the tissues and DNA to relax, expand, and replicate to begin the healing process which our body naturally knows how to perform. Learning this information about DNA reinforced the importance of relaxation for our bodies. Relaxing helps to heal from injury and to recover from all activities that work our physical systems.

Later I read an article that DNA is activated by light. This made perfect sense to me as I had been using low power LASER for wound healing. The light increases ATP and mitochondrial function in a cell. I began to contemplate angels and their influence in our world. I feel angels as emanations of light. When people feel or see an angelic presence in their lives, they are experiencing the vibration of light. What does this do to their DNA? I guess depending on their reaction, whether it is love or fear the experience either relaxes or contracts their DNA. This would set up a cascade of either healing or resistance in their systems depending on their beliefs and state of their nervous system.

Now in this time when I equate love, light, and breath as all one and the same energy from the Universe, what is happening with our DNA? We are bringing in greater and greater amounts of high frequency light on to the planet and we are activating the non-coded DNA to begin the process of becoming a multidimensional being capable of activities that we previously assigned only to masters, gurus or avatars. We are now in a timeline that we are each being given the opportunity to allow more light and more love into our systems. This is happening whether we are consciously allowing it or not. Although, when consciously creating with the light, it magnifies its ability to expand within us. It comes down to either allowing and relaxing or resisting and contracting which is ultimately our own free will choice. Ease and grace or pain and suffering, our choice.

The water experiments of Masaru Emoto[ii] showed the effect of human consciousness on water crystals. He shows examples of human feelings creating either beautiful or ugly structures in water that has been frozen and viewed under an electron microscope. This is important to consider because 75% or more of our bodies are composed of water. Every cell in our body contains water. Does the water we consume and use in our bodies carry a vibration of love or fear? Is the water in our body filled with positive emotions of love, hope, faith, and peace or negative emotions of hate, worry, and fear? Is the water in our cells filled with love and light vibration to enhance the activity of our DNA or are we full of heavy and dense constrictions that limit the flow in all areas of our bodies?

These ideas are worthy of much contemplations as we choose how to lead our lives. It is our choice to be relaxed or to be contracted, to be accepting and allowing, or rejecting and resistant. This applies to everything in our life. The science of epigenetics tells us we are affected by our environment continually. We are the environment in which our cells bath and DNA functions. We can choose to love ourselves and create the optimal environment for life to heal, expand, and grow. We can choose peaceful music, calm trusting reactions to situations, seeing the beauty in everything especially ourselves, and loving ourselves even when we falter. We can laugh more, dance more, and smile more for the miraculous adventure life is.

May we all enjoy expanding and relaxing in life.

Personal Power

"You have power over your mind - not outside events.
Realize this and you will find strength."
Marcus Aurelius

Reflection on peace requires having an understanding of my relationship to personal power. Let's start at the very beginning of my life here on Earth. I came into this life with a mission, a blazing light-filled entity with a desire, hope, and dare I say, purpose. Needless to say, as with all of us separation created forgetfulness and it was a shock to be here and encounter the power struggles that exist every day. Born in the early 60s, I became deeply conditioned in the authoritarian, keep control, and dominate everything model. I abandoned my emotions as too messy and uncontrollable. I became completely baffled when they did show up and what to do with them. I succumbed to the big people's authoritarian model and remained small, lost my voice, and remained quiet in the face of adversity. Any personal power I had, I betrayed by not believing in my intuition. I became a strong, in-control girl ready to make her way in the world the only way she knew how. I may have tried to dominate my dogs; they never really listened. I may have tried to boss around my friends, but then we were all playing the same game. I did control my inner landscape and essentially never treasured who I am or allowed the sensitive soul inside out to play, especially in public. I was embarrassed when my tears welled upon hearing a piece of music; who knew it was my tender heart loving the moment. I was shocked when anger arose and I immediately looked to release it in avoidance ways; who knew that cardio exercise could change energy. Facing any emotion and actually cooperating with it so that I could come into harmony was unheard of during my early years.

My dominant, authoritarian model began to shake loose as I entered my career. This is where I learnt that any semblance of power, I thought I had over another's action was a joke. I could tell Mr. Jones what to do, how to do it, and how often to do it. I could demonstrate and I could write it down, but at the end of the day if Mr. Jones was going to participate in his exercise program or not was his decision. This was shocking to little "Do what you are told" me. It appeared that some people did exactly what they wanted to do no matter the consequences. They blatantly ignored health instructions and simply carried on. They often using every trick in the book to convince me and themselves that their course of action was fine. My initial reaction of shock and horror led to a laissez-faire attitude. I did my part giving them all the exercises they needed and what they chose to do or not do was none of my business. I stopped taking it personally when they did not follow my instructions and accepted whatever happened. Over my 30 years of client care, I would say that developing alignment with my authentic inner power allowed me to accept each person for who they were and love them just like that.

My power evolution continued and moved closer to home. Marriage is a shared cooperative relationship or chaos ensues. My personal preferences seemed to work on the little things like socks into the laundry hamper and cleaning up the dishes. When bigger issues loomed on the horizon it became essential to understand each other, share, and find loving solutions together. This all worked out well with an educated consenting adult so the next challenge of my power management style arrived in my life as children.

My children have been my greatest teachers. They triggered every emotion in my system. They made me laugh, cry, and seethe all at the same moment. How they did this was miraculous, God knew what he was doing making children. I love them so darn much and they can play my buttons in multiple tunes. My eldest, bless his soul, took the brunt of my authoritarian model. He simply would not allow it to deter any of his actions and carried on his merry way doing exactly whatever came into his curious, imaginative mind. Once I was juggling three children and living life in the fast lane, I realized that there was not a hope that I had any power over them. They were each light beings of their own making masquerading as my children. They had far more power over me than I did over them. I remember cringing as my youngest innocently told Grandpa a tale I had hoped would never be repeated. When I tried to control any situations, I became contracted and defensive. I simply had to let go, trust and flow with events as they arose. Our household life was unpredictable, messy, and beautiful which gave my children the opportunity to grow into their potential and express who they came here to be.

Contemplation and meditation led me to my authentic power, my soul self. My inner power first and foremost meant accepting all parts of myself. Loving every aspect of me with adoration, understanding, patience, and joy. This has been a moment by moment ongoing practice of self-love and appreciation. This has involved diving deeply into my inner world to feel all my emotions arising, to accept myself as the human being I am and hold myself gently when I do not like what I see. This has been a cultivation of understanding, cooperation, clarity, and reverence for my life.

Self-love is gratitude for being here as I am and caring for myself. In these states of being, I find my authentic power arises and I feel my connection to myself, everyone, and everything. I know myself as the love and light that I am as I live conscientiously. I sense a peace that passes all understanding and in that peace is a knowing that this is where truth and harmony exist. Each of us is hard-wired with this same authentic power. The question becomes how have we been conditioned to forget our authentic power and believe in another's story of power. When I can see the story that has been created then I can rewrite the lines. I can move into a new story that is aligned with my soul and expressing my soul qualities in my personality now. This is the heart of the matter to know ourselves well enough to know that our soul is guiding our actions in the world. When each of us, or enough of us, can carry this soul frequency then new solutions to old problems will evolve into our world. My inner power is your inner power showing up in a different costume playing a different part and always connected to the same source energy of Love.

Today, I know my personal power is being a sensitive, loving soul and I respect who I am. My world is a place of relative peace and harmony which creates joy, love, connection, and trust in life. I allow the powerful loving energy, I am and we all are, to create the age of peace that is emerging. I know that my internal soul power is my guiding light, my GPS, and with it in the driver's seat I know the ride will be unimaginably wonderful.

May we all infuse the world with our loving and peaceful presence to spread light into the darkest corners.

May peace prevail in each of our hearts and minds to usher in the new golden age with deep reverence and joy.

Beyond Imagination

"What is now proved was once only imagined."
William Blake

When I was in my mid-forties, I returned to dinghy sailing after 20 years away. My children were involved in the sailing race team and I was invited to joined them. I trained with the team, raced, travelled, and found myself continually doing things that I would never have expected. In my wildest dreams, I would never have guessed that I would be trapezing off a 14-foot dinghy travelling at high speed. Yet there I was thrilled, exhilarated, and courageously enjoying the wonders of skiff sailing. Also, I was participating in a sport alongside my teenagers. I can honestly say, I never imagined such an opportunity could happen. It was a privilege and a delightful time in my life especially sharing it with them.

We are here, on planet Earth spinning around our Sun in a galaxy somewhere in a Universe, right here and now being human in all our perfect imperfection. We are part of that vast presence and we are our own unique self. As humans, we usually want to have our finger on every pulse, to know exactly what is happening and the influence it has on us. The alternative is to humbly surrender to whatever is happening and accept that we are a grain of sand in the vastness of The Mystery. A deeply adored and precious grain of sand supported and guided along our trajectory. The design of life is far richer than we can imagine and we have to learn to trust that. I have come to believe that The Universe always works for me providing me more than I can imagine. I have often heard that when asking The Universe for something the statement, "This or something better" should be added, just in case I am limiting the possibilities. I do not know what lies ahead and I have the choice to trust or to worry. Time and time again my life has shown me to trust that The Universe has a better plan than I could imagine in my humanness.

In the past, I wanted to control and force life into my vision to give myself a sense of security. One of my challenges has been controlling my emotions. Those unsightly reactions to life so quickly judged by the outer world and by my inner critic in all its protective glory. Energy in motion, emotion is a range; a scale and I wanted to control it all. I rarely allowed out the over-the-top, cell bursting joy that I felt when I was connected to nature or seeing the reconnection of souls. I hide the smile too big, the tears of appreciation of life, the knowing faith that this is who I am meant to be and the body bouncing ecstatic state of being fully who I am. I did not want to let out the fire-breathing dragon that lives inside that wanted to roar at injustice, tear apart false belief and create havoc in an attempt to change the status quo. No, no, I wanted to control all of it and appear on an even keel. On top of all that is occurring, being in the neutral safe zone.

In my experience that safe zone created a stagnation like swamp water. There was no flow and all the colours in the crayon box disappeared. My creativity was stifled if not completely obliterated. Being solidly in control created walls and meant not being alive to the wonders of life. Life lost its spontaneous nature if I held the reins too tight. I became separated from my essence, my nourishment, and my raison d'etre when I grasped, held, and attached to having to know everything. My true desire is to be a fully alive soul having a human experience here on Mother Earth, our home. I want to know my connection to all I am; the good, the bad, the scared, and the jubilant. It is all sacred and I want to be free to express it in vibrant colour and ecstatic motion. I feel deep compassion for all of us as we each live our daily experiences on this planet of duality to the best of our abilities.

I first heard the term "Both And" from a dance workshop with Kathy Altman[iii], it means to hold the full duality of life and allow more that could be. This has become an expansive way for me to hold opposing dynamics in life. Later, we were relating our experiences during a circle

32

time and were instructed to add at the end of our sharing, "And that is not all of me". This emphasized that I am telling my narrative and I know I am so much more. This acknowledgement allows a door to open for magic and beyond our imagination events to happen.

I want to be connected to the stream of life that pulses in each cell of my being. I want to feel the urge of evolution motivating my action. I want to dance with all there is the sunrise, the sunset, the day, and the night. All of it an endless pulse of creative vibration surging throughout absolutely everything. Is it messy? That depends whether we see dirt as glorious fertile ground or as something that needs to be cleaned up and removed. Is it risky? That depends on our level of trust in ourselves and our trust that life has our back even if it does not look like it from our limited perspective. Does it take courage? For sure, to express ourselves in all our glory is not the box that the human cultural control system has in mind. It is a glorious connection to ourselves, to life, and all our potential. Each of us gets to choose our way of believing life is for us.

In my view, we use control to separate ourselves from the part of ourselves that is completely, forever connected to life and the juice of creation that life is. Each of us has a choice, to let go of control and fall into trusting. We can choose to be connected, alive, and emotional or to keep control, stay rigid, and separated from our true nature. While horse riding, I learnt that the reins can be held in tight limiting the horse's capacity or they can be held loosely to give the horse its natural freedom. I use this visual often as a touchstone to remind myself to relax and allow. It is really all about learning to love ourselves whole so we can accept everything. Then we can be free to enjoy the journey of this lifetime in full connectivity to life, pulsing grace and ease into everything. We can upgrade our connections and unplug from control systems. Control is an illusion of our own creation. I have never seen the season not change, a child not grow or a mood not shift. It is all illusory, fluid, infinite vastness in which we dwell. Let us be the creation we are, arising from that infinity. All is divine, vines connected and intertwined. Feel the unity of our nature in each breathe and praise the glory of our presence here, now, and everywhere.

May our imaginations soar and our trust in life rise as we love ourselves.

Love

Piglet: "How do you spell 'love'?"
Pooh: "You don't spell it ...you feel it." A.A. Milne

Love is the ocean current running deep. Love is the warp and woof of the tapestry. Love is All That Is. Love is the Alpha and the Omega.

Love is so much more. Love is the container and the contents. Love is the swirl, the swish and the pulse of life. Love is the dance and the dancer.

We are Love. Love is the basic building block of life. We are life living. We are love living. We are life living lovingly.

Love is an elemental and intrinsic nature of creation. Love is a truth emerging like a flower blossoming and wafting its fragrance in its radiance.

Love has always been understood by the poets, the painters, the musicians, and the mystics of our world. They express their creations attempting to catch the essence of Love's beauty. They capture our imagination with a phrase, a curve, a colour, or a melody. We are held mesmerized and woven into the magic of love.

Love is seen in the gentle touch of care for another. Love is seen in exchanges with eye contact and tender recognition. Love is seen as children grow and move into their lives. Love is seen in playgrounds, at bedsides, and in beaming smiles.

Love is seen as the leaves of autumn are released from the tree. Love is felt in the soft blanket of snow that falls on a calm winter evening. Love is the warmth of the sun in spring warming the ground and our hearts. Love is the soft summer rains and the long days of light. Love is the dedication of seasons to return again and again.

Love is in the new, the in-between, and the old. Love is everywhere and everything.

Love is invisible like a light until it penetrates the dark. Love travels in our lives mysteriously, the undercurrent below the undercurrent. Love is the palpable peace that passeth all understanding.

When I forget all the above, I think of LOVE as the Light Of Vitality Everywhere. It is a light that ignites vitality all around us. Vitality is the strength, the passion, and the expression of life being life. Vitality is the expression of the light teaming with life. Teaming with LOVE.

Love is our natural state. Love is our unified oneness of being.

Love is our core being whether we choose to reveal it or not. We have the choice to allow love to flow into us, around us, and through us emanating into the world. We are conduits of love here on Planet Earth.

I have acknowledged more and more that I am love. My life has become filled with more and more love, peace, and joy. I am the spacious, quiet opportunity for Love to emerge. I am the faucet through which love pours forth. This is who I am.

May we all know who we are.

Grace

"I do not at all understand the mystery of grace – only that it meets us where we are but does not leave us where it found us." Anne Lamott

I have been blessed to feel Grace present. It entered unannounced and filled all space inside my body and the field around me. It was a moment treating a client who was suffering from the anticipation of her mother's death. Something she said allowed Grace to enter and speak through me. I have no idea what was said. I do know that the client was moved deeply and we both were aware that Grace had visited.

Grace is The Mystery bestowing a blessing on us. It arrives if we can be spacious enough and carries us forward on its wings of love. It is divine will presenting itself. It is our higher self stepping in fully for a brief visit.

When she appears, I have a sense of my human self stepping aside, to allow.

It is not in my power to force the arrival of Grace. For me, power is my will to make choices, accept responsibility, and show up in whatever is arising. It is creating boundaries, giving and receiving respect, and honour for my self and others. Grace arrives. Power is a choice, especially how it is wielded. Hence the power to love is a human choice, while Grace is love on the wings of the divine.

It takes courage to be open to Grace happening. In my experience, it takes the willingness to know myself and love myself in every moment. It is stepping into the world fully exposed, hiding nothing, and accepting everything. It is being open and wholeheartedly patient with whatever is arising. It is accepting that there is no thing to change. It is allowing and stabilizing the love energy as it moves in space. It is being vulnerable, waiting, listening, and staying rooted in my own influence and not being swayed by that which surrounds me. It is being grounded and connected to my human self and allowing space for the divine to circulate as it will. This is the courageous stance to allow Grace to enter.

Grace is said to be seen in the way a person walks, interacts with others and moves in the world. It speaks to me of being an honourable, noble human being aware of sovereignty and aware of oneness. It is moving with lightness and humour through the trials of our human existence as best we are able. It is knowing we are so much more in our divine expression. As a human to be graceful is creating the space for Grace to move in the world.

May all beings know themselves as Grace having a human experience.

Death

"To everything, there is a season and a time to every purpose under the heaven. A time to be born, and a time to die…" Ecclesiastes 3.1

I spent a summer with my mother as she was dying; she did her life review with me each day sitting in the garden. I had a one-year-old, life seemed to fill his every action as it diminished in her. The summer was exceptional for Nova Scotia, long hot days with lots of sun, and the garden bursting forth with new surprises each day. Each day she seemed a little further away, she never seemed to fear death, but then she was always accepting of everything in life. One late summer day when the clouds moved in and the omen of autumn was upon us, she passed from this life. I was with her moments after her last breath, but she was no longer there; a shell of flesh and bone lay before my eyes. I had had time to say my good-byes so this moment was a blessing, a release. It was later as we left the hospital that my true awakening began.

There was an opening in the clouds that was rimmed with the gold of the setting sun. I felt the angels guiding my mother's spirit into the next realm through this golden gate. I then realized that death is not the end of life, but a new beginning, a different stage and not to be feared.

Our fear of death and how it limits our ability to embrace a healthy and peaceful life is a worthy contemplation. Death is a subject much tabooed in Western culture, we rarely discuss our emotions around death and we certainly do not prepare people to embrace death as a part of life. We are often shocked when death occurs, deeply grieved, and ill prepared to handle the mechanics of a person completing their life. It is with great sadness that we say good-bye to our loved ones and we mourn their passing. Can we celebrate the life that has brought joy and love to the world and now transforms into pure energy? How does our fear of death affect our ability to live? Can we honour the dead and the living by respecting all choices? Can we accept that we will not live forever and keep our lives in order, to ease the burden of those that remain?

The fear of death allows us to deny our lives, limits our vision, and traps us in our fear of the unknown. We race through our lives trying to reach materialistic goals often forgetting those around us who are here to share relationships. Sudden changes in perspective such as a terminal illness force people to step back and look at their lives. We are all a part of nature. We are born with nothing and we will die with nothing. So why are we here? We are here to form loving relationships and enjoy the process of life. If we are scared to experience parts of life for a fear of dying, we will never find the courage to leap during opportunities.

People who experience a near-death experience show us life beyond death. These people experience calm and peace while moving away from the body toward a light. Then a moment comes when they consciously appear to choose to return into the physical body vehicle. These people often make new choices as to how they live their lives after this experience. They often embark on a renewed path of love touching the hearts of many.

I have read about Indigenous customs that have different perspectives on death. Some believe that physical life can end with a deliberate, conscious release of our spirit. Techniques are learnt which allow a soul to choose when they will return to a non-physical state. The day is chosen, the life of the person is honoured and celebrated. Then the person shuts down their bodily functions and their soul leaves the human body. A true acceptance that our energy goes on forever and we can embrace both life and death.

If we make peace with dying, then we are fully aware of our energy and ready to dance with life. Eastern beliefs teach us to be prepared to die at any time. The concept that death walks beside us always as we are living can focus us on the essentials of life. We can close our circles with love and not leave words unspoken or desires unfilled. We can simplify our lives to give our time to the relationships we value. We can walk in nature with respect and thanks for the joy there is to behold. We can open our hearts to love. We know love is what we leave with each person we touch or nurture in this life. We need to feel the courage to accept that death is a transformation, not a fearful finale.

May we all know death as a cycle of life.

Part 2 - Dancing with Life

K nowing that we are much more than the biology which we inhabit here on this planet of duality and action, I have learnt to recognize my soul in action. Knowing that I am a magnificent being who co-creates with the creative forces and laws of the universe, I dance with life. I came to this life to reconnect people to their truth as souls having a human experience. We are so mired in the quicksand of our lives we disconnect from our soul urge then we are diverted from our soul path of grace, gratitude, and joy. Our purpose is to bring experiences to the One which we all come from and return to. This requires partnering with life in an intuitive flow of harmony and balance.

In this section, I bring forth the ways that I dance with life. My choices that I have made to live a life of joy, love, and peace. This is my path and yours will be uniquely yours. May my experiences bring ideas, confidence, and contentment to you as we all dance our unique path. We are always together, connected and sovereign.

May our dance with life be filled with joy.

Healthy Body Healthy Mind

"When you arise in the morning, think of what a precious privilege it is to be alive – to breathe, to think, to enjoy, to love." Marcus Aurelius

We humans are funny creatures. Most mammals grow up quickly and can meet their survival needs rapidly. Foals get their feet under them and are walking in the pasture very soon after birth. We, humans, are dependent on our caretakers to feed us, keep us warm, and tend us in every way as a newborn and for years after. The frontal lobe in the human brain doesn't fully develop until age 25. We enter helpless, only expressing our needs and discomforts and we grow slowly into caring for ourselves.

How do we learn to care for ourselves? Do we consider our physical, mental, emotional, and spiritual state as we care for ourselves? Caring for yourself is loving yourself.

47

It is you, meeting your needs for sleep, food, water, hygiene, space, exercise, support, comfort, and creativity. So many people put others before themselves and end up creating disease in their systems. As a physiotherapist, I often had to say to clients, "You can only care for others if you care for yourself". The same applies to love!

There are so many ways and paths to follow in personal self-care. Being consistent and walking the middle road has been my way. I tend to develop routines that are simple and easy to apply in my life. Regular meals, regular exercise, and regular sleep. I wake up and spend a few minutes gathering myself saying my prayers or intentions for the day. I wash my face and feel love for myself as I look in the mirror. I dress in joyful colours and comfortable clothes. I eat wholesome foods that are mostly homemade and created with love. I do a variety of exercises with a consistent foundation of aerobic, stretching, and core exercises to support all my different activities. I make sleep a priority and use a relaxation practice to settle at night. I enjoy the day to day with gratitude and satisfaction that all is well.

My dad would have a quick nap after lunch before heading back to work and again after dinner. I smile, remembering when he started to snore one of the dogs would climb on his chest and bark at him. His rest was short and effective. During my busiest years of owning and working in my physiotherapy clinic as well as raising our children, I followed my dad's example and napped. It was my saviour, I worked in the morning, had lunch, and settled in for a 15-20 minute power nap. Then I would be off for the remainder of the day's tasks. This afternoon reset renewed my energy and vitality to flow with the hectic years of a busy household and clinic ownership. It was a lifesaver. I began napping in university. In the evening, I arrived at the library open my books, lay my head down in my arms, and napped for 10 minutes. Refreshed I proceeded with my studies. Power napping has been a healthy life skill for me.

I have been a meditator for twenty plus years. This has been my place to find calm and solace. It has given me tools to contemplate, breathe, connect with myself, and view life from a detached place of acceptance and peace. When I was a physiotherapist, I would be washing my hands between clients. Each time I washed my hands I pretended that the water was flowing all over me cleansing my energy field and grounding me into Mother Earth. I would take some deep breaths to clear my mind, to refresh my thought, and clear my mental field. This allowed me to be ready to meet the needs of my next client, to be focused and mindful.

Healthy emotional expression has taken me years to learn. In my family of origin, I simply ignored emotions, buried them, or denied them. It was when I was raising my kids that I had to look closely at what was buried inside by me. I found myself angry, frustrated, and overwhelmed. I needed to learn and see where those emotions were coming from. This began my journey of self-discovery which is an ongoing process of loving myself every day in every way. Emotions are still an area that many of us tiptoe around not knowing what to do, how to be, and how to safely express ourselves. For me, acceptance has been the first step and courage to allow myself the right to feel what I feel. My difficulties with emotions become obvious with any conflict and in times of fatigue. Now, I make conscious choices as I express my feelings while being respectful and considerate to myself and others. This often takes me a little time, so I step back and summon the courage to say what I need to say or do what I need to do. Trusting that a mindful response will be more aligned than a knee jerk reaction.

As a culture, we need to learn to feel. Our society brings us up in a frenzy of doing by creating a whirlwind of constant activity. The essence of simply being is lost among the rush around. We are always striving and running after the next shiny object. All of this push is created by the mind. We tell ourselves I need to, I must do, and I should have. It is exhausting. It leads to anxiety and overwhelms us. It has us talking about how stressed out we are like it is a badge of honour. It has convinced us that being stressed is normal and the only way forward. Truly, pausing, stepping back, and slowing down allows a much healthier approach to everything. When we reduce our need for goals and start to consider how we want to feel day to day a whole new world opens up. A world that includes our interior life as well as our exterior life. We begin to make our inner state a priority from which we create our lifestyle.

Danielle LaPorte's[iv] work called *Desire Mapping* asks us to create goals based on how we want to feel. Can we choose to create our lives with goals such as feeling peaceful, feeling lighter, feeling connected, and feeling open? Can our desires be joy, boldness, authenticity, and courage? This approach is moving our focus from the mind to the heart, the emotional center, the feeling center of our body. This increases our awareness of what the heck we are feeling and how we can change the feeling by making new choices in our lifestyle and our mindset. This is not about avoiding the busy lives we have; it is approaching our day with a plan of how we want to feel. When we start our day intending to feel peace, love, and joy we lighten the density of our world.

This is not about denying our unappealing feelings. It is acknowledging; this makes me angry and takes me away from the calm I want to feel. What can I do to calm myself even briefly so that I can deal with the anger that is rising? Can I take a couple of breaths, do I need to walk away for a moment, or take a walk outside in nature? My desire is to feel calm how can I regain that state instead of making decisions and taking action from this place of anger. From a place of calm, the anger can be acknowledged and I can inquire why the anger arose and what it needs from me. I often remind myself that this is my feeling, my anger. It is mine to become acquainted with and to evaluate how much belongs to me and how much belongs to the collective energy field. This approach to my emotions has been the gift of my contemplative life and has been a keystone to my healthy body and healthy mind.

May we all feel our truth and respond with love.

Beauty Everywhere

*"Never say there is nothing beautiful in the world
anymore. There is always something to make you
wonder in the shape of a tree, the trembling of a leaf."*
Albert Schweitzer

The appreciation of beauty that surrounds us is a choice. What our personal self finds beautiful varies widely as we are each unique. Some of the things we consider beautiful are culturally conditioned and others are our quirky selves. I believe the act of appreciating beauty, in whatever manner we see it, is the key.

Beauty is stopping and taking in a piece of artwork, a photo on a brochure, or graffiti on a wall. It is listening to music or to poems. It is hearing the leaves rustling on the trees as the wind dances through. It is appreciating the light as it kisses our cheek. It is tasting sweet ripe fruit in season. It is touching the soft delicate skin of a baby or the soft fur of a puppy. It is smelling the honeysuckle, the rose, or the jasmine. The gift of the human experience is to see, hear, touch, smell, and taste and it is a beautiful privilege.

All our senses enliven with beauty. Beauty calms our nerves, allows us to take a deep breath, and helps us stop even momentarily to align ourselves with our spirit. Beauty that surrounds us brings us into a deeper relationship with the world we live in. Appreciating the beauty around us opens us to acknowledge the beauty within us. Every one of us is a beautiful creation, we are so similar in how our body is constructed and then we are so unique in our appearance. The diversity is stunning and awe-inspiring.

The hidden jewel in each of us is the beauty of who we are and how we are in the world. There is immense beauty in how people touch one another. The gentle kindly caress of a hand on a cheek. The hand on a shoulder to encourage and support. The head nod of agreement. The eye contact of acknowledgement. Some beautiful greetings are huge bear hugs, others, subtle nods of approval. The beauty of the human body running, dancing, making music, and any activity shows the miracle of ability. Beauty is the energy of our spirit we are willing to share with the world.

Our words are energy in motion. We have the choice to speak into the world with beauty and love as our intent.

We influence the world by speaking with clarity, gently and concisely, or loudly and obnoxiously. Considering if we speak with beauty or not is a worthy contemplation. What words do we choose to express ourselves? Are they rough curses, or gentle balms of kindness? Our words can cut a person deeply. Each of us needs to consider what words we place out in the world. Our words can create chaotic disturbances, or calming smoothness in the energy field that surround us. A momentary pause for a deep breath can allow us to choose our words wisely and lovingly.

Our homes can be places were beauty can flourish. The colours we chose to surround ourselves with create atmosphere. Levels of cleanliness and tidiness vs dirty and cluttered impact our moods. Our homes are a reflection of ourselves. My home is spacious with little clutter and light that dances through it as the sun makes its daily journey. I have interesting things and memories to delight my eyes and recall joyful experiences. This has not always been so as five of us lived and grew in this house. Then it was a hub of comings and goings and contained all the stuff of family life. Truly its own chaotic beauty with much less concern about tidiness and much more on functionality. Now it is our place of renewal, peaceful and beautiful.

We make the choice in every moment whether to create beauty or not. Mother Nature creates beauty everywhere and we can follow her lead. Honouring our own inner and outer beauty expands love in the world. It is an aspect of loving ourselves wholeheartedly. May beauty flourish in all.

May beauty be seen and acknowledged as love being expressed.

Choices

An old Cherokee is teaching his grandson about life. "A fight is going on inside me," he said to the boy. "It is a terrible fight and it is between two wolves. One is evil – he is anger, envy, sorrow, regret, greed, arrogance, self-pity, guilt, resentment, inferiority, lies, false pride, superiority, and ego."

He continued, "The other is good – he is joy, peace, love, hope, serenity, humility, kindness, benevolence, empathy, generosity, truth, compassion, and faith. The same fight is going on inside you – and inside every other person, too."

The grandson thought about it for a minute and then asked his grandfather, "Which wolf will win?"

The old Cherokee simply replied, "The one you feed."
(source unknown)

This Native American parable speaks directly to our ability to create with our choices. Do I feed love or do I feed fear with my actions, my words, or my thoughts? Do I follow my heart brimming with love and trust in life or do I follow my mind filled with voices that fear everything?

My choice is easy. I desire to lead my life from love as love. I have learned to drop into my heart and the center of my body to feel the vibration of love emanating from my core. This aligns with the research of the HeartMath Institute[v] which shows us that the electromagnetic field around the heart is larger and more powerful than the field around the brain. A greater field of energetic influence comes from our heart's activity moving into the world than our mind's activity.

My center of being is not simply my physical heart. I focus on my central core as my deepest connection with The Mystery. This shift seems to lessen the influence of the emotional charges that reside in my heart from past traumatic events and conditioning. I locate my core in front of my spine inside behind my belly button. This area is called the "dan tien" or "hara" center. There are many names; the important part is to feel that you are in your center, whatever name or image you use. It is this central core from which I can feel loving, healing energy radiate.

How do I stay in my core, stable center? I have three C's that I focus on and use as a saying. I say, "My mind is clear, my heart is calm, and my body is comfortable," as I take several deep cleansing breaths. Deep slow abdominal inspiration, in through my nose flowing oxygen into my lungs as my belly expands. I visualize the air entering into every cell of my body from the tip of my head down to my toes. Then a slow expiration through pursed lips and I visualize all tension releasing from my system like arrows moving away from all parts of my body. I visualize breath, light, and love from the universe mixing together entering all aspects of my being clearing, calming, and comforting.

Once I am centred and focused then I can make my choices and feel confident that I am following my heart and feeding love. I am a visual person so I use my mind to see myself drop from my head above down into my center. I use the mind to create the strong intention that love will be my guiding force in all my decisions. I feel the change in my body, the sensory shift in my center, where my energetic vibration is arising from. I ground myself by dropping cords of light in various colours into the heart of Mother Earth to increase my stability and comfort in my body. The body is a part of the earth made up of the same molecules and atoms so this is a calming technique. I also acknowledge Mother Earth for all her gifts with deep gratitude.

I use these centring and grounding techniques first thing in the morning. I include the intention to feel fully connected to myself and the earth's energy throughout the day. I take the stance of slowing down, breathing, finding my center, and grounding whenever I feel knocked off balance physically or emotionally. Whenever I am in the shower I center and ground. The water clears away residue from dreamtime or daily life that remains in my energy field. Then I can set an intention to be clear, open and grounded in the pure energy I am.

In my experience, the fear of the unknown has been the greatest force to swirl me into my head. The uncertainty of what is next and the anticipation of what is coming toward me. We collectively tend to think of the future with a negative bias. We anticipate that negative things are more likely to happen than positive. This unknowing can hold me in a straitjacket of limitation, unable to move ahead, desperate for a change from what is occurring, hopelessly confused, and ungrounded. The only recourse I know is to center myself, slow down, breath, and simply sit with all the swirling. I do not make decisions knowing that I am in a swirl. I do my best not to judge and criticize myself for being in this place once again. Ultimately, I use all my techniques to love myself. I embrace the pain, the fear, and the uncertainty with a blanket of loving energy. I understanding that it is my mind trying to protect me and keep me safe. I let my open, loving heart's energy calm the confused mind, helping it to move into a positive outlook, a more trusting life. I connect to feeling safe by imagining angels encircling me. I thank my mind. I appreciate its concern and fears. I lovingly tell it that I am choosing a new course of action that is brave and comes from love.

Each of us makes so many choices along our journey some we may regret and others we are grateful for. Our freedom to make choices is a gift we should appreciate. Sadly, it is a gift that is not available to or not chosen by all humans. When we are faced with choices and have gathered the pertinent information we can sit with our options. In contemplating the possibilities, we can make decisions with clarity, honesty, and consideration for ourselves and others. My style is to sit and visualize the possibilities and feel which course of action warms my heart, lights me up, or invokes a yes inside my core. Then I have a clear path to follow.

It is always wise to sleep on a decision before taking action. A good night's sleep can bring clarity and resolve. By making time to have one more look in the light of a new day we can often see more clearly. It can take the sting out of our reaction and it can calm the need to rescue another. It creates space to let things be and makes for wiser choices.

Years ago, I learnt to use a pendulum to help make choices. Then I learnt to ask my physical body for a yes or no response. Now I can feel my energy expand or contract as I contemplate options. This is useful for being tuned into my system and what is my best course of action. I check in when I am buying something, deciding what to wear, choosing foods, and many other small and large decisions that I make every day. These techniques are based on energy and have served me well as I have navigated my life choices.

A pendulum can be any weighted object at the end of a cord. There are fancy ones and simple homemade ones. A pendulum needs to be programmed, which simply means holding it steady and asking it to show a Yes, show a No, and show a Maybe. It will do so by swirling in one direction or another for each. Then it is ready for a question which has a Yes, No, Maybe answer. As always forming the question is key.

To use your body as a pendulum stand, ground yourself and ask your body to show a Yes, show a No, and show a Maybe. Your body will sway in a direction for each response and then you can ask your question. These techniques are simple. They do take practice and faith to follow them. My experience is that it takes the guesswork out of life. What top should I wear today, which earrings, who should I hire for this job, the possibilities are endless. I have used these techniques for years. Now I can feel the energetic Yes or No in my body. I have become more aware of the subtle body responses to my questions and follow the answers with confidence. I use these techniques daily. It has been fun to train myself by using them while shopping or picking what I will wear. I am always confident that I am making the best choices for me. I always trust that yes is yes, no is no, and maybe is a no for now.

Years ago, my husband was planning to leave the military because we did not want to move. I asked my pendulum would he be leaving the Navy. It said No. I asked several times intermittently since this was a new tool and my faith in the answer was low. Every indicator in the outside world was that he would leave the Navy. My pendulum kept saying No. A few weeks later a resignation opened up a position that kept him in the Navy for another three years. My faith in my pendulum and the world of energetic response rose and has assisted me with my choices ever since.

May all our choices come from consideration.

Forgiveness

"For all eternity, I forgive you and you forgive me."
William Blake

Forgiveness is an important act for us humans. It is always recommended and may or may not be acted upon. Some would say that everything is in the perfection of the divine and forgiveness is not required. This implies that all acts which appear against us were of our own design before we were born. The concept being we made contracts with those in our lives to act in the play of our life just as they have done, are doing, and will do. Once we enter the veils of being human, we no longer remember the creation of the plan or the reasoning behind it and live as we do. Thus, we collect wounds that we blame on others and often on ourselves. Hence forgiveness becomes a path through these human predicaments.

One method of forgiveness and reconciliation comes from the Hawaiian culture. It is called Ho'oponopono, meaning to make right. I consider it as adjusting my energy to develop harmony within myself, with other people, and to places and things. This creates a right relationship meaning it facilitates energy between two beings to align with acceptance and allows peace to flow between them. I do not claim to fully understand this as it originates from another cultural heritage than my own. I have used it personally to reconcile many personal issues and relationships. This is my experience of which I speak.

The practice which I use is to state, "Ho'oponopono, I see you in me and I see me in you" which is recognizing our Oneness. This honours how we all carry the same experiences and are here all the same and unique. I follow with the words, "I am sorry, please forgive me, thank you, I love you". Then I repeat the process several times until a shift is felt within my energy body.

I use this technique to resolve my inner charges around people and situations. I visualize the particular person who in my mind is causing my distress then I begin the process. I have used it to seek forgiveness from my own younger self who I abandoned along the way of growing up. I have used it in a global sense when I perceive injustice or desire to introduce the energy of reconciliation to a situation. I have used it when I have seen unkind treatment of animals.

In my experience, using Ho'oponopono is me taking responsibility for my part in what has or is happening. I sit here searching for a simple example. The universe always provides. I am outside writing and the chickadees are flying around. One just pooped on my shirt. Now my true reaction is to laugh, clean it up, and carry on. Another reaction would be to get all indignant and curse the wee bird and coil myself in anger or why me, this always happens to me, frustration. To make right, I would have to see that the bird is simply like I am, doing what birds do as I am human doing what humans do. Then I would use the words, "I am sorry, please forgive me, thank you, I love you" to bring peace between us. I am sorry that I reacted the way I did, can you forgive me my outburst, thank you whatever your response, I love you just as you are. I would repeat the process looking inward to the part of myself that got tied in a knot. I would say I am sorry you got knotted up, please forgive me any part I had in creating the knot, thank you for being you, I love you as you are. I am owning my part and accepting what happened without judgement. Life happens.

I do this practice for my own peace and serenity with life. I am not trying to change another. I am changing inside me. I am identifying that my own grievance is causing me harm by contracting my energy. I bring contemplation and love to it to smooth the energy and create greater flow in my life. The effect on the other person is truly not my concern. When I free my energy to flow with greater ease and grace then all of life benefits because we are all the same, one energy.

May we all allow forgiveness for ourselves and others.

Balance

"He who lives in harmony with himself lives in harmony with the universe." Marcus Aurelius

W e live in a world of duality. We walk a balancing act as we navigate our lives. The Chinese yin yang seems to describe it best for me. Everything is two sides to the same coin. A curve has an inside and outside. Both are present to create the whole, and within wholeness, both are occurring.

The act of balancing our lives is so essential to peace and progress. We need to have action and we need rest. We need to work and we need to play. We need time together and we need time alone. I have chosen to walk a middle path, enough of this and not too much of that, always dancing the line between.

Balance in the physical sense has always been important for me. I learnt to balance on the blade of an ice skate and to trapeze on the edge of a small sailboat. I rehabilitated balance in clients so they can safely step ahead. I taught doing enough to create change and not so much to hinder healing. I balanced my career and family. So much of life is the art of balancing. I still love to walk along the beach, balancing on the logs.

A fundamental level of balance is balancing the masculine and feminine principles within ourselves. We each wear our outer suit of gender whatever that may be, and within we have active the feminine and the masculine principles, the yin yang working within us. Beyond this planet our energy is androgynous, we are both female and male spiralling together as one. We can sometimes see this as people age, they become less defined as either one or the other and seem to balance both within. The history of patriarchy and matriarchy in our world says that one or the other is better or dominant. I am much more inclined toward a balance of both. I am personally grateful for my masculine side of becoming, the aspect that brings intention into action in my life. I am equally grateful for my feminine side of being, the part that creates potential and allows space for intuitive flow. Both are vital to my overall state of being. I am always delighted when I see feminine in my masculine or vice versa. It is the dance of yin yang ever in dynamic motion weaving within each other and always a part of the whole. Words are difficult to find to convey this truth. It appears in my dance as I approach the oneness I am.

The exercise, that follows, has helped me with the discovery and exploration of my masculine and feminine sides. It has helped me to balance these elements within. It is equally useful to hold any duality that is truly part of the whole. As examples: light/dark, heaven/earth, right/wrong, good/bad. May you enjoy the contemplations that this exercise can bring forth. I have developed this technique from verbal guidance I received from Sharon Leslie[vi] many years ago.

Technique - Alchemy of Duality to Unity Meditation

Specifically exploring inner masculine and inner feminine principles of balance. It is useful for any duality in life.

Hold your Right hand out palm up. Ask that your inner male energy be brought into your Right hand. Your Left hand is resting palm down on your leg or behind your back.

Focus on this inner masculine energy which is you.

Is there an image of your inner masculine energy? A colour? A temperature?

Are there qualities that stand out?

Can you say hello and converse?

Now reverse. Hold your Left Hand out palm up. Ask that your inner female energy be brought forth into your Left hand. Your Right hand is resting palm down on your leg or behind your back.

Focus on this inner feminine energy which is you.

Is there an image of your inner feminine energy? A colour? A temperature?

Are there qualities that stand out?

Can you say hello and converse?

Take as much time as you need to be with each energy individually.

When that part is complete bring the Right hand out palm up with your inner masculine energy present. Allow your inner male to look at your inner female. Equally, allow your inner female to look at your inner male.

Consider their relationship with each other.

Has your inner female as the keeper of a vision shared it with your inner male so that he can manifest the vision?

How willing is your inner male to honour, accept, and respect your inner female and her vision?

How willing is your inner female to show up, support him, and nurture him in his activities?

How willing is your inner male to send appreciation to your inner female and vice versa?

How willing is your inner female to acknowledge your inner male and vice versa?

Take all the time you need and always feel free to return to these dialogues.

Now image a rainbow spiral slinky between both hands, between these two dualistic energies, between your inner male and your inner female. These energies are dancing together as lovers of life. Call in your highest embodiment of each of these energies into the appropriate hand.

Observe any changes in the images or qualities.

Holding the fully embodied energies of the two principles now join your hands together allowing these energies to come together in The Mystery. The beloved and the lover, the heart and the ego, the subconscious and the conscious mind.

Meditate on the power of The Mystery to bring forth new creations. Fresh ideas that honour both the feminine and the masculine contribution. Trust that together they can ride the magic carpet of love in life for the highest good of all.

Place both hands together over your heart and feel the wholeness within yourself. Feel the feminine love of the masculine, feel the love and honour the heart has for the ego. Know your wholeness and your magic in togetherness, Oneness. Breath in love and breath out love deeply connected across all time and space. Namaste, I bow to the divine in you.

When I first did this exercise, it gave me much understanding of what was going on inside me. My masculine energy rode in on a steed, very powerfully then he deflated and became small. He was exhausted from carrying the actions of my life without any acknowledgement of his great work. He looked at her and did not pay any attention to her. My feminine energy was very ethereal and wispy not overly present and she had no awareness of his presence or his sacrifice to keep my life rolling along. She was not supporting his actions with her nurturing energy at all. Creation is born from the feminine principle so I began there and I invited her to come into my life with a great presence and involvement. I focused on giving myself time to dream, to be in nature, to dance and to make space for her to participate in my life. Gradually she became a strong force and I felt her like a queen. A queen is in service to her people with fierce love and delight for life. I reclaimed my feminine power to be soft and strong, kind and firm, flowing and present. Now when my queen looks at my masculine, she sees his devotion to protect her and his commitment to take action. She is acknowledging and appreciative of his stance and ways. In her gratitude, she sends flowing loving energy to him so he feels nurtured and sustained. He is no longer deflated and nor does he need to prance around trying to be everything to everyone. His energy is more grounded and consistent. He is the king of my life, serving all his people with devotion and impeccable brilliance. Now when he looks at her, he sees her majesty and he is heartened that he has a companion to support him while walking this journey. He is attentive to her needs and supports her creational force and ways. Today my feminine and my masculine walk together along the rainbow bridge each grateful and supportive of the other. Hand in hand being love in the world.

Recently, I was doing some healing work via journeying on the drum. During the healing, I was removing daggers that were lodged in my right side. As I was doing so, I realized that all these daggers were on my right side, my masculine side. My masculine energy had taken the brunt of all these daggers allowing my feminine side to remain free and clear from the wounds. Tears flowed with love for him, how he had protected her and allowed her the freedom to be while he held the trauma. It was incredibly healing. Always moving into great wholeness, she is being and he is becoming, together.

The yin yang teachings and symbol speak to the intra-relationship of the feminine and the masculine principle throughout everything. The play of each intertwined with the other always influencing life as it spirals forward through time and space. The imbalance between the masculine and the feminine on this planet will be healed by each of us balancing these forces within our own system. The patriarchy can not be sustained and the divine feminine is flooding our world to correct the balance. The work that follows is the type of changes that bring forth unity and equality.

One day during my morning meditation I became aware of a huge energy in my aura, very agitated energy. I happened to have an acupuncture session that day during which my body requested an esoteric session for clarity as well as the Bach Flower essence of holly. When I got home, I looked up holly to discover it is a remedy for envy, jealousy, resentment, and hatred. I had the realization that the energy in my field was all the negativity surrounding the masculine. I went and picked holly and a rose for my sacred space and I journeyed. The journey on the drum was incredible, a multitude of women were in my healing garden and energies came in to heal all the old stories. I felt the old stories drop away, holly came present and radiated its remedy to all from the middle of a circle. Then a huge golden citrine crystal appeared. All of us present placed our hands on it. I became very hot as the energy was transmuted. All the women energetically present sat back into relaxation and then men from my life and historic figures appeared. I did forgiveness with each one. A huge leather book appeared on a stool. I closed and latched the book as it contained all the stories of the past no longer of service, each sister present seemed to have done the same. Then eagles came in, took the books and flew to the sun. Then we relaxed on the beach and cleansed in the oceanic waters. We live in powerful times. I deeply honour the balance of the masculine and the feminine in each and every one of us with the deepest love for all.

May we all know balance and walk in unity.

Trusting the Unknown

"In the universe, there are things that are known and things that are unknown, and in between there are doors." William Blake

We humans are moving into greater wholeness of unity consciousness. In our becoming, we are widening our embrace of Oneness. This includes integrating our mystical nature or divine nature with our human nature. No more separation. We are no longer one or the other, we are the totality, all One.

This can be seen as you are me and I am you. We are woven from the same cloth into individualized expressions of All That Is. We are in a time of major shift as we return to love as our base starting point of everything we do.

I have been contemplating my reaction to the unknown as I journey forward into these writings for a book. How can we be comfortable trusting the unknown? How can we settle and allow The Mystery to offer us step by step a path to tread upon? A path that we cannot see. Yet we are asked to trust the path like we use our headlights on a pitch-black night. We only see a short way ahead of ourselves at any moment. We relax and move along steadily trusting life.

My contemplation has moved deeply around trust. A few years ago, when we were skiing there was cloud fog at the peaks of the mountain. The visibility was terrible. I felt fear rising. Losing my companions, getting hit by another, not seeing a mogul, and a multitude of other fears. I called my spiritual allies to guide me forward and help me relax into the experience. Then I set off trusting the path, a bit slower and cautious yet confident that I was safe. This level of trust has taken me years to realize and can become precarious in new unknown situations. For me, the ability to take some deep breaths and remain calm has been essential in moving forward with trust.

Now I am sensing the becoming of my next potential in this life and yet the path is misty and unclear. How do I step out, take the proverbial leap off the edge of the cliff? This has been a question I have held with curiosity for years. The only answer I have is trust that the universe and all of life is for me. I am supported and held with the deepest love and caring as a human being. I am enough, all I do and how I do everything is enough.

Being enough and knowing deep in my core that I am enough has been a lifelong journey. My childhood left me in a people pleasing pattern. My worth was based on whether others thought well of me or my creations. I valued what others thought more than I valued my own opinion of myself. I lacked trust in myself.

On my path, learning to trust my own intuitive nature was primary. I learnt to trust that the information I get is valuable. That I need to speak up when I feel it is time to do so. Trusting my knowing has been life changing. I can now say that "I know that I know what I know". My energetic intuition is my GPS of life. I listen to my gut, if it is wobbly, I ask for help understanding what is happening. I listen to the subtle signals which I have learned to discern as valuable information for my way ahead.

Trusting the unknown reminds me of when I first bought my physiotherapy clinic. I was aware that the clinic, very close to my home was for sale. I explored the possibilities of purchasing it and concluded that it was more than I desired to get into at that time. Then a few months passed and it became obvious to me that I could make this commitment and still raise my family with my naval officer husband. I look back now and all my experiences with the clinic were incredible and fostered growth. I see how much courage it took to make the purchase and step up to that level of responsibility. I see how I relied on my organizational skills to keep the clinic and my household on an even keel, along with help from friends. I also saw how my physiotherapist skills developed along with my confidence. My trust in myself and my intuitive knowing came online in a greater capacity to assist with the healing of clients. As I assessed a person's condition, I would open myself to becoming a question mark. This essentially made me open and curious as to what was happening and ultimately gave me information as to what was occurring in their body. This information integrated with my education and past experiences created a course of action to assist their healing. Another vital learning along the way was to be content to say "I do not know". This was big for me to accept that I do not know and I was still valuable not a failure. I also opened to my curiosity to add that I would happily research the question or consider the predicament.

I am forever grateful that I am a curious being. This continues to allow me to explore new frontiers. Presently I view the world from an energetic stance as well as a physical, mental, and emotional one. This expands my potential and possibility as I live in a greater field of awareness that includes the energetic influence of the field, we all inhabit. I am also a routine being. I have stable foundational practices that keep me firmly grounded in my human nature and life on Mother Earth. I tend to my needs with devotion and delight.

One of my routines is my prayers. These may end up being brought forth when I first wake up, as I walk or ride my bike, or brush my teeth. Truly any time it works for me works. Some days they are condensed to the simple words "Thank you for everything". Other days I immerse myself in a process that sets my intentions and energy for the day ahead.

My prayer process contains words that I may or may not speak aloud as well as visualizations and colours that accompany the words. I imagine this happening and visualize through out the prayer each activity the words are prompting. It is a dynamic interactive creation sourced from love for myself and all. Here is a prayer process I use regularly.

"Dearest beloved I Am presence, please strengthen the roses around me and ground them deeply into Mother Earth consciousness. Please help me to stay centered in my center and fully connected to the source of all that I am and fully grounded into the heart of Mother Earth. Dear Mother Earth, I allow you to fill me with your love and protection."

As I am saying the above words. I am visualizing four large roses all around me that send their roots deep into the earth. I visualize a cord of light coming from above into my center and one from my center to the center of the earth. I see and feel the love coming upwards through my legs then overflowing like a fountain filling and clearing my whole aura. This is followed by seeing vines wrap around the four roses and hundreds of thousands of unground multi-coloured roses placed in a spiral around the vines for anyone who needs a packet of loving energy without touch my system. This is my form of protection that is always present around me. It is soft, loving and generous when people meet my energy. It is also an energetic boundary.

I continue asking the universe. "Please fill me with our divine knowing, our divine feeling and our divine consciousness so that I may move forward in my journey radiating divine light, divine love, and divine healing. To be all that I can be for the highest good of all." This sets my intention of how I will be for the day.

I follow with asking for blessings. "Mother Goddess, Father God bless my spirit, bless my soul, bless my physical, mental, emotional and etheric bodies. Bless my hands and actions, bless my words and bless my thoughts. Let me come with all I am, to honour all that is. In peace, in love, enlighten."

Then I review all that I am grateful for in my life. I have a routine of gratitude that I created and enjoy. I will often begin contemplating something that is arising in life and sending loving intentions to its outcome. My practice soothes my soul, aligns me for my day or drops me into a peaceful state for sleep at night. I have created my practice for me from elements that resonate with my heart and soul. We each can create our own way of interacting with our divine nature. There are as many ways as people on the planet. The most important element of prayer, in my mind, is to infuse it all with love. The love and devotion to life, truly heartfelt and expressed, creates a love factor that can change the world.

Through mystical experiences, I have come to realize our ultimate oneness. I have found myself merging with various masters. We are them and they are us has become an experiential truth for me. This has augmented my trust in how much we are loved by them as we are all One. There is no true separation only a perception of such to allow our human nature to exist and to make our own choices of experiences through free will. As we evolve, we discover our wholeness as human and divine, all One.

I am an embodied soul. My soul which is my mystical nature is present here and now in my human body, showing the way forward into the unknown. I am creating my life from love and unified theory to bring forth the magic we all are. It is exciting, and requires continual trust in what is.

May all beings trust their path into the unknown by resting in the present now.

Kindness First and Foremost

"A single act of kindness throws out roots in all directions, and the roots spring up and make new trees."
Amelia Earhart

K indness is defined in the Oxford dictionary as showing friendliness, affection or consideration. Synonyms of the word "kind" are to be gentle, compassionate, generous, and warm-hearted. The word "kindly" implies a sympathetic attitude towards others and a willingness to treat others with considerate behaviour.

For me, kindness is the caring, gentle behaviour that considers other's responses to my actions. It encompasses respecting and honouring another for the simple reason that they too are a human being doing their best in life. It allows each of us to hold the innocence and pure nature of another in the light of their highest potential.

Can we hold another gently in a sweet embrace of caring and consideration? Can we be gracious in our thoughts, words, and deeds? Can we be all of this for ourselves also? Can kindness start at home, in our own being, body, and family?

When I act from a place of kindness and compassion, I respect myself, I feel grounded, and I am centered. When I act with any other background flavour to my action, I feel off-center and ungrounded. I find myself trying to figure out how to admit my regression and mend fences.

Kindness is the gentle act of feeling and thinking through what your actions create in the world. Kindness takes courage, strength, and discipline to evoke in the world. It takes stopping and having a breath before acting. It takes extending ourselves out to gain knowledge of what another will feel. It is a practice, a way of being in the world. Can you and I contemplate being kind in our world for ourselves and all others?

Kindness means moving into the world with an open, vulnerable heart focused on the consequences of our presence in the world.

If everyone allowed kindness to be the platform from which they leap, this world would transform before our eyes.

May kindness lead all our actions.

Allowing Joy to Flow

"I would love to live like a river flows, carried by the surprise of its own unfolding." John O'Donohue

I believe joy is our natural state. I like to call it the Juice of You. The innerness of you, me, all of us that flows in our veins, our meridians and throughout our being. The energy that brings a smile to our face as we ponder life. The brightness that we feel when we see a newborn or a puppy. The goodness we all are in our purity.

When life is always orientated toward seriousness allowing our innocence out to play becomes essential. The adult stuff we all encounter every day can stifle our desires to tap our toes or guffaw at a joke. We are beings of balance; too much of anything one way or another means we lose our footing on our path. Being silly comes naturally to children; they think nothing of it and move on when the moment is past. We as adults tend to lose our silly beans along the way. Dressing up, imagination,

85

laughter, and fun for no good reason are ways to allow yourself some silly moments.

When a dear friend had her birthday party. She invited us to bring our inner child and play along. It was brilliant. I took the opportunity with glee, dressing up, doing my hair in braided pigtails, and participating in all the games she organized. Later that evening as I sat quietly under the stars, I felt completely utterly satisfied and open to life. My inner child was completely content as was my adult self. I could feel the balance of all my needs being met. I smiled deeply and felt the joy of a life lived lovingly.

I remember sitting around the kitchen table with the kids doing riddles and jokes, all of them simple, silly, and creating laughter. On occasion, I played simple songs on the piano and the kids danced around the living room. The freedom to be and the joy of movement spreading good humour all around.

I am grateful for my children that they rekindled silliness inside me; even when they grew and began to mock me when I was silly. I was on a mission to allow silliness a place in my life. I let loose the constraints of adult life by dancing, laughing, and imagining which brought forth joy. When I embrace joy, I bring it everywhere I go.

Remembering that I am joy helps me to stop and smell the roses or any beautiful flower that gifts us with such delight of scent. Right now, the honeysuckle is blooming and wafting in the wind. It is simply heaven on earth, what joy to behold and smell.

The joy of seeing people I have missed in my day to day life is especially heart enhancing. The warmth and juicy feelings of sharing a hug and letting my heart mingle with theirs for a moment. The delight of someone arriving feeling the joy of connection. The inner smile of excitement and pleasure. Truly, we all love to be loved and seeing someone sparkle because we arrived in their space is a gift of love and appreciation. Our hearts expand with being adored as precious. The pure joy of sharing life with another.

This brings forth a lesson I learnt from a friend many years ago around hugs. It is about arm placement while hugging and the message it sends. If you tend to hug by putting both your arms over the other person's shoulders the message is "I need your support". If you tend to put both your arms around their waist the message is "I will support you". If you wrap one arm above and one below you are indicating balanced sharing of support and heart energy. I have adopted this balanced style for years and find it has a marvellous heartwarming effect. Throwing one arm up and one arm down as I approach a person opens my heart and expands my energy. When I am embracing them, we are making a heart to heart connection. There is lots of room for a peck on the cheek, even both sides if desired. I feel that this style honours myself and the other person allowing us each to stand in our own energy while celebrating our friendship as open and balanced. Just thinking about all the wonderful hugs, I have shared, makes me smile and joy fills my being.

Choosing to smile is a relaxing healthy approach that spreads joy in the world. We never know when a smile will lift someone into a brighter day. The facial muscles get exercise by smiling. Smiling makes me feel lighter inside. Smiling allows me to spread my light. Smiling as I go about my day can improve my mood. The simple joy of being alive is something to smile about and tends to have an infectious quality to shift into lightness. Smile and laugh whenever you can for the health of it.

Smiles, lightness, and laughter let our innate joy out to play and enliven life. Intend for it to be so. The joy of being alive, breathing, moving, dancing and loving life. So much wonder and awe.

May we all know joy in our heart.

Being Light

"Then my heart with pleasure fills, And dances with the daffodils." William Wordsworth

When we are able to be the light, can we see how we bring ease to everything that arises? Can we see how our light is the only light truly present in all?

This is a memory that reminds me to focus on lightness. We were on our sailing vacation when I was twelve years old. I was hanging out at the marina watching some adults trying to walk on the water with Styrofoam pontoons that they stepped into. It was amusing as they continually ended up swimming. I decided that I would like to give walking on water a try. I approached them and was happily permitted to use the pontoons. It was awkward to get into and to move the pontoon as I had to slide my legs forward and back. I did walk on the water and had a fun time. Being light allowed me to walk on the water.

Be light and do not sink into the water. Water can be referred to as an emotional element of the collective consciousness. The message transforms to be light and do not sink into the emotional fields of others. Then I was physically light, now I am asked to be emotionally and mentally light so as not to sink into dense moods and mental traps. When I allow a mood of seriousness to replace levity, I can find myself becoming fatigued and confused as the energy becomes weighty. An attitude of lightness allows me to stay afloat in day to day life.

This is a great metaphor for life. When we stay light, we can navigate life with greater ease. When we burden ourselves with heaviness, we risk sinking. To travel light is to move with greater speed and agility in life, especially in a busy airport. We need to lighten our load, carry around less baggage physically, mentally, and emotionally. Our heavy bags are often filled with pain, physical aches, emotional turmoil, and mental anguish. The more we accumulate these various pains the more weighted down and dense we become. How can we lighten our load? By making more space we can stay afloat and enjoy life every day.

In my world, choosing to be light is the first step. We can imagine ourselves as a hot air balloon floating along then releasing what no longer serves us. Who does it serve to hold that old grudge? Who does it serve to be angry? When we are angry at someone or something, it is our blood pressure which rises. The other is unaffected, our stuff is our stuff to change if desired. We all accumulate baggage as we travel through life. If we deal with stuff as quickly as possible then we do not need to carry it around forever. When we are light enough to see what is weighing us down, we can accept our role in events and initiate change. We can relax our judgements of ourselves and others, allowing energy to shift and move. We free ourselves, no longer needing to be weighed down and heavy. We stay light.

There are many ways to raise ourselves up and be lighter. Music, exercise, nature, meditation, and relaxation to name a few. All these wonderful things can make space in our system, can change our perspective, and can lighten our load. We can become like a featherweight floating in life drifting on the air currents allowing everything to be as it is.

We know that we are energy and light is energy. We can imagine ourselves as shining our light, beaming waves of light outward, and bringing brightness into the dark. I use the image of a lighthouse shining into the dark of night to guide vessels to safe harbour. When I see myself as light my view expands and I allow much more to simply move through my system and not get bogged down.

Being light allows us to hold things gently, not taking on other's burdens and heaviness. Seriousness is a shadowy place that never cracks a smile or laughs at itself. We can take things others say lightly not personally. Truly be light never taking anything personally, this is such an important stance in life. Being light means not judging ourselves or others. The sunlight shines equally on every single one of us, with no judgement and no criticism. Be like the sunlight and shine your light equally with everyone and everything.

We are all light. We can shine in our world or we can hide our light. It is our choice.

We can move in life as lightness or we can plod along weighed down by our seriousness. Our choice always.

May we all know and love ourselves as the light we all are.

May we dance with life lightly wrapped in joy.

Part 3 - Knowing Ourselves As So Much More

Knowing ourselves as so much more is expanding into The Mystery and the world of energy. We are beings of energy. Energy that goes by many names including light, love, chi, or prana to name a few. Moving into exploration of these areas of energetic reality opened my world to healing, mystery, and magic. I explored acupuncture, reiki, shamanic journeywork, and energy medicine over the years. I live a rich inner life connected to multi-dimensions traversing time and space. I lead an intuitive life based on my energetic choices. I am clear, connected to All That Is, and allow The Mystery to flow through me. I am grounded, realistic, and sensible. This is the balance of the middle road I walk as a divine human being. What follows are essays of my way with energy and diving into the mystical.

May we all enjoy life beyond the ordinary reality.

Messy Tangled Energy

"There is nothing either good or bad, but thinking makes it so." *William Shakespeare*

Struggle today! I am feeling like a flag being buffeted by the wind, nowhere to go, simply endure. Why is every day is different? One day I awaken feeling together, organized, aligned with life, content, happy, and satisfied. Another day, today, I wake up discombobulated, uncertain, doubting my value, feeling the day ahead as a vast expanse of coping alone, nowhere to go, and nothing to do.

Years ago, I had so much to do and so much to organize. I just kept going. I answered all the demands of others. This is not the case now as I no longer work as a physiotherapist; I am retired. My children are grown and we are officially empty nesters; it was a thirty-year process. I have forgotten the hard bits and miss the fun interactions, and daily sharing of their lives. The renewed life of my marriage is a joy. My husband is still working at a high demand position that has fun moments and repetitive high stress. His retirement is approaching, which will be a new level of freedom, and another transition for both of us.

Life is one transition to another. Change is the only constant. Of course, this can be seen from a negative or a positive vantage point. We can fear that change is going to take from us, or burden us with more. We can also accept change with an attitude of "This too will pass" and the sun will shine tomorrow. I thought it would get easier so that at some undefined point I would no longer feel all the emotional energy that I do. That one day I would no longer tumble back into my personal anxiety about myself. That one day I would feel satisfied that who I am, how I am in the world, and what I do is perfect for me. That this undercurrent of "You should be better, more and different" would vanish. That this critical voice of "You are not good enough" would run out of ways of saying the same thing over and over. Alas, I like many humans have an inferior ego which is an amazing performer and never misses an opportunity to act out its part. Some days life is more of a roller coaster and the transitions are sudden and terrifying and other days life is an inner tube ride down a lazy sunny river. Each day is a new one and each will pass away into the new beginning of the next day.

Where does our inferior ego come from? It has a long history of creation. Some of it is created through our parents and our ancestral lineage. We do inherit the ways of the past. Some of it from our own spiritual lineage. Some of it is laid down in utero. The events that impact our mother during our nine-month journey inside her influence us. Then all that happens to us as young children when we are in the sponge stage of development creates tracks and patterns that are the foundation of our beliefs about our selves and the world, we live in. Then lo and behold, when we are in a situation similar to that which created the original track, the jingle begins to play in our head, and we are caught in the perfect storm of not loving ourselves. The swirl of confusion, loneliness, disappointment and frustration takes over our view and all appears hopeless. The concept that these beliefs are no longer true has no impact, we feel caught in an unchangeable pattern.

What can we do with this dismal view? We had no control; these bad things just happened. Often, we do not even remember them happening. Sometimes they happened so frequently we blocked the memories of all the non-love. This is such a loaded basket of limiting beliefs that can drag us down into the sewer of life. If we let it!

We do have a choice! We can become completely overwhelmed by our thoughts and emotions. Or we can choose to become curious and look at where they have come from and why they are showing their faces today. Gratefully, I am a curious person and love learning about human relationships with myself and others. Why are we the way we are? Why am I the way I am? This question has led me on every quest that I have ventured along including these writings.

Can we acknowledge that our lives have been a product of many patterns? Remember there were positive beliefs as well as negative that came into our system. Can we accept that somehow, we accepted to enter this life knowing that what happened would happen? Could we imagine that we had a plan for our lives before we were born? That we have chosen the circumstances that we experience, so we can grow toward more love not less? Can we allow new possibilities so that we can create a fresh outlook of our past and what happened? Can we be open to healing what arises when we are triggered by events and slip back into old patterns? Can we see these events as our chance to get curious and give ourselves more love than our small one ever felt when these patterns were instilled in us? Can we take our pain and transmute it into loving kindness for ourselves? Is this easy? No! Is it worth it to create a life of greater calm, ease, and peace? Yes! Do we have to nitpick every little thing that ever happened to us? No! The more loving acceptance we can generate for ourselves at all stages of life helps to ease the depth of these tracks and to lay down new healthy ones. This is truly rewiring your brain to activate higher energetic states of peace, love, and joy. Science is providing us with more and more evidence in neuroplasticity and neurophysiology that changes are always possible in the brain. The exciting advances in brain research and how our neurological system can influence our physical and emotional biology is very exciting and gives us all a ray of sunshine. We are not stuck with the beliefs that we received without even knowing it. Everything can change! This is exciting and gives huge amounts of hope for ourselves, humanity, and our world.

So, what happened that made today feel like a struggle? Well, I watched a documentary film last night about people doing incredible feats of physical adventure and read about others whose humanitarian efforts are amazing. It fanned the flames of negative thoughts. "My life is dull and boring." "I never do anything exciting." "Also, I am no good because I have not saved the world today." True or false doesn't really matter, the smouldering coal was enlivened in my system. Besides, I am alone all day as my husband is away on business, the hours ahead felt vast and empty as my obligations are only to myself. Then began the chant, "You have so much privilege and time, you should do more, and be more appreciative" the drumbeat of lacking worthiness. The critical symphony became a cacophonous roar and pulled me out of loving myself just as I am and trusting that life is unfolding perfectly.

Fortunately, while writing and contemplating these areas of life I have brought self love into my life. I have smiled at myself and loved me for exactly who I am as I am. I have smiled the inner smile at the same old tunes playing on repeat. I have lived my purpose to bring lighter and higher vibe energy to life. Today my energy needed a boost. Now, I am feeling energized and excited. I will jump on the treadmill for a run, my exercise routine a couple of times a week. I have something to listen to and expand my knowledge. I have a couple of things that will take me out into the world to interact with others and shine my light. I will flow along with the day, steadily trusting what unfolds. A day of bits and pieces that make me smile and feel that I wholeheartedly belong. I am grateful for this process and the reminder that I get to choose. I am grateful for the many tools in my toolbox that keep me on a path of lightness and love. I am grateful that I am more and more accepting that my contribution and service to the world and the universe is to simply be who I am. Being my clear loving self, bringing my vibrational energy with me where ever I show up.

I am deeply grateful that I believe in myself and perhaps this is the gift that my childhood gave me. I had to learn that I am valuable, deserving of love, and worthy of my own love first. Learning to love myself has truly been the key that shifted my life into greater ease and grace. I only struggle with old ideas and beliefs occasionally now. There is an easy relatively fast return to my truth when I am knocked off-kilter by life.

Learning to love ourselves as the grace of divinity that we are. This is a huge accomplishment for every one of us. It is the road less travelled in the past. It is now the leading edge of creating change in our lives and the world. It is a new way of being. It is fresh and needs to be refreshed continually. Being an avatar of love is a newness that takes courage, renewed faith, devotion, and discipline to follow the path. The path of love. The path of love no matter what appears, to meet non-love with love at every turn. Quite frankly the most difficult one to walk this path with is ourselves. May God loves us while we learn to love ourselves. May we learn to pick ourselves up when we fall and allow love to lead our way always. When we fall into doubt may we stay open to receive love. When we need some time to wallow in the murkier emotions of life, we can love that too. Love is the only answer.

May we all believe in love.

Meditation

"The Universe is change: our life is what our thoughts make it." Marcus Aurelius

Years ago, I began meditating. It became obvious to me that I needed a practice to calm my overwhelmed system. I owned a physiotherapy clinic, treated a dozen clients a half-day, had three young children, my husband was at sea frequently for extended periods and my father was ageing. I began to meditate because I needed calm and serenity within my full-on days doing life.

A friend and I took a meditation course at the local recreation centre. This introduced me to a variety of forms of meditation with the central theme of mindfulness. I committed to giving myself 20 minutes every night sitting on my pillow. The kids were in bed, the tasks of the day complete and the prep for tomorrow done. I bought a CD of meditation music and sat being aware of my breath. I let myself sink into the center of my being. No matter where my mind wandered or how much I wiggled by the end of the time in quiet solitude I felt calm and connected to myself.

Through the years, I have continued this practice with many variations. I have used deep relaxation body scanning techniques to let go of tension. I have listened to brain balancing CDs that promote the theta and delta brain waves which move our system into relaxation and rejuvenation. I routinely wake up and give myself from 5-30 minutes to lie flat in bed and simply be with my breath. At the end of the day, I once again lie flat in bed and review the day with gratitude. I have said my prayers riding my bike to work or while walking the dog. I breathe slowly and deeply to prepare to be courageous. I have danced my prayers. I have travelled on the drum to do shamanic healing. I have explored many ways of healing and connecting to the world beyond time and space. I consistently return to the simplicity of slowing down, breathing, and being mindful of what is happening inside me. This mindfulness is my ongoing practice throughout the day.

When I treated clients, I would take a breath before entering the cubicle. This included an intention to leave whatever had happened just prior behind and to clear my mind to be receptive to the needs of this person in front of me. Every time I washed my hands, I visualized light entering my system and clearing away any debris that needed to be released. These small habits allowed me to stay grounded, open, and prepared for whatever arose next. They also allowed me to be open to my inner guidance system, my intuition, with clarity and confidence. They helped me to listen attentively to each person. My dedication to these ways has brought ease and grace to my life that flows along with relative simplicity and magic.

The practice of loving myself has enhanced all my ways. I can now stand in front of a mirror and say, "I love you and you are beautiful inside and out". This has been quite a journey. The initial attempts felt like fake it until you make it. Eventually, I could imagine that I was saying, "I love you" to myself as a small child and that allowed me to be more authentic in my expression and I could feel a shift inside me. Now I can confidently say, "I love you" and include my whole self, now, then and future me. This can be seen as deeply parenting my inner selves to accept that I am worthy to be love, to be loved, and to be loving. These practices have opened the door for me to be more loving to myself and others. They have allowed my love and light to shine ever brighter into this world. I am deeply grateful to Matt Kahn[vii] and his work called *"The Love Revolution"* for guiding me into loving myself. During his workshops, he teaches saying, "I love you" to yourself and repeating to yourself words that you wished you had heard as a child. In my case, I chose the words, "You are delightful and you are welcome here". This reminds me that I am the light and my light is welcome. These simple techniques have opened me to profound healing.

This all sounds easy in writing and I can tell you it has been a journey. My mind was a super list maker, dinner planner, idea machine whenever I sat quietly. The best advice was simply to let the thoughts pass like clouds. When I discovered I had gone way down the rabbit hole into planning a whole event or renovation I would simply acknowledge myself, allow myself to let it go, and return to my breath. My tendency towards perfection was challenged here. The pain in my body while sitting was real. The inner critic muttering that I was wasting time was persistent. Gratefully my devotion to being mindful and calm in life kept me returning to my center, breathing in love and breathing out love.

My journey has had many obstacles as that is the nature of our human experience. I have lived the lows of loss, death, disappointment, abandonment, helplessness, and the medley of human encounters in relationship to ourselves and others. I have also ridden the highs of exhilaration, the joys of success, the wonders of life and love, and the mind-blowing delight of feeling totally connected to everything. The ups and downs have all been stabilized by my practice of being mindful and aware of myself as I am living life lovingly.

I am grateful for meditation, contemplation, and mindfulness as they continually align me with my truth and joy of life. Richard Rudd[viii] has written a delightful book called *"The Art of Contemplation"* which explores this subject in depth. I highly recommend it.

May we each find our own way to bring peace into our lives.

Nature Nurtures our Soul

"Come forth into the light of things, let nature be your teacher." William Wordsworth

My mother would hustle me outside saying, "Go change the air in your lungs." I have always loved being outdoors. In the garden, I dig into rich fertile soil. I watch as new sprouts emerge from the earth into blossoms of gorgeous colours. I treasure the water that nourishes all of nature including us. I bask in the warmth of the sun like a snake. I observe what birds are flitting around the yard. I listen to the wind in the trees. I follow the stars and the moon as they parade across the night sky. I feel my soul connection to The Mystery when I deepen my awareness of what is happening in the natural world all around me. I am enlivened by spending time in nature everyday.

Being outside in nature means being exposed to the elements. The elements that are part of us; the building blocks of our body which are earth, water, fire and air. Being aware of nature connects us to the cycles of the seasons. It means knowing and accepting ourselves as a part of that cycle. We humans are in the same cycle of birth and death as everything on Mother Earth. She is our home, on which we thrive, thanks to all her gifts of food, water, and shelter. Our connection to the natural world feeds our truth, our essence.

Sailing has been a huge influence in my life. The experience of being on the water, feeling the sunlight and being moved by the wind cleanses my aura and rids my mind of any cobwebs. It leaves me refreshed and clear to step ashore in a new attitude. Sailing dinghies requires constant attention and adjustment that brings me fully into the present moment. In the Now moment, I enter the flow with nature, then a rhythm is created with the elements. The results are awe-inspiring and exhilarating.

Allowing nature to be our teacher bears beautiful fruit. By observing any part of the natural world, we are taught valuable lessons to apply in our lives. The trees are continually changing, teaching us about cycles and ways to be. In winter, they rest, quiet sentinels of the landscape. They whisper to us. They say to rest, wait and let your roots grow. In Spring, they show their beauty with flowers and leaves sprouting with the message of renewal and possibility. In Summer, their canopy shades us and their fruit ripens. They share their gifts of abundance happily. In Fall, they give us a show of colour and release their leaves. They teach us how to be less attached to things and simply let go. The trees are beautiful teachers that connect heaven and earth. They speak to our soul in their own love language.

Water brings lessons of trust in change. The element itself changes from solid, to liquid then to gas. It moves from visible to invisible. The rain cycle lets us see water pour on to the earth then it integrates by joining the streams, rivers, and oceans then it mysteriously returns to the sky hidden in clouds ready to return again. We gain much knowledge by contemplating these cycles of water and what they show us about our lives.

The ocean holds lessons in her tides. The tides come and go in their cyclical patterns aligned with the gravitational pull of the moon. The land does not insist that the tide show up at the same time each day. The land allows the movement of the tides to proceed in its natural way. We can remember this as we insist that people behave in certain ways. Maybe they are not naturally able to be as you would like. We need to trust that they are doing their best, and as with the tide everything changes continually. Change is the one constant in the world. By observing, we see how we are always changing.

When a weather storm is upon us, I can feel the intensity in my body. Everything is on alert. I love being cozy inside, listening to the wind in the trees, the powerful sweep of nature through the land, and the rain beating on the skylight. The world is enlivened with anticipation of strong energies moving. The storms teach us to honour Mother Nature, she is powerful and deserves respect. Observing weather storms helps us adapt to stormy times in our lives. We can take heart that storms always come to an end. We can learn to adjust our sails to how the wind is changing in all conditions. We can be adaptable and flexible, allowing ourselves to bend in the storm, instead of being rigid and at risk of damage. In our lives, when we can stay flexible, we can ride difficult passages with greater ease.

In August 2017, I saw the totality of the solar eclipse. Nature doing its thing. It was an awe-inspiring event which merits sharing. The mass of humanity that came to witness the event and the logistics for a small town to handle the influx was mind-boggling. We stayed in a tent city, glamping. The comradery that develops in these atmospheres speaks volumes about the truth of human nature to co-operate and share resources. On the day of the event, people were milling around, setting up telescopes and cameras, and sharing stories of past experiences. Everyone is prepared with filters so they can look at the sun. Then the moon, passing between the earth and the sun, begins to take its first nibbles, and then bites out of the sun. About fifteen minutes before totality the air changes, it gets cooler and quieter, the birds stop singing as if dusk is arriving. At the moment of totality, we saw a phenomenon called Bailey's beads. This is pink round light beads as the sunlight is passing through the hills on the moon. Suddenly it is dark and the stars are visible. Yes, they are there in the sky all the time. We logically know this to be true, but seeing stars at ten fifteen in the morning, wow. Looking at the moon covering the sun reveals the solar corona which looks like bright wispy filaments coming off the sun, normally invisible due to the brightness. Then as the process continues and the moments of total coverage are arriving and ending, there is a phenomenon called the diamond ring, where a ring of light surrounds the moon and then a point of brilliance as the sun is being exposed. We saw it at the end as the sun was returning. The whole experience was mystical and moving. I lay on the ground with my binoculars that had special filters feeling the approach of totality. As the darkness fell, I found tears rolling down my cheeks. I felt magic that words can not describe. A palpable feeling of the mysterious awe of life being experienced, so expansive. My love of nature and life flowed forth. That humans once found these events terrifying makes perfect sense. I am so grateful for the science that brings an understanding of the mechanics of eclipses. Still The Mystery was present and palpable as well.

I have shared ways that nature nurtures my soul. I am continually in awe and wonder. I watch the development of humans. I gaze at the colours of sunset dancing across the sky. I feel the magic of the betwixt and between time of dawn or dusk. I ponder the moonlight as it plays hide and seek in the trees. I am enraptured as all my senses are enlivened by contact with the natural world. My soul dances in delight as I enjoy the treasures of creation happening. Being alive is a miraculous wonder-filled experience of sensual delight. May your soul be nurtured by nature everyday.

May you see all that is unfolding all around you everyday with awe and wonder.

Know Thy Self as Love

*"The only thing of importance, when we depart, will be
the traces of love we have left behind."*
Albert Schweitzer

To know thy self and to love thy self are powerful statements of intent. They set us on a journey of exploration opening our curiosity about our mind, our heart, and our soul. This is the journey I have taken to exploring consciousness. It has led me into my understanding of energy, intention, and life.

I am an aspect of The Mystery expressing through this body, mind, and heart having experiences within a space time continuum. The One source consciousness animates all our personal selves. The sacred penetrates everything. My willingness to have an open heart grants me eyes to see the divine at play throughout life.

I am Love fully, completely, every bit of me as we all are. I receive love from everywhere; it is all Love, so I am loved. I am loving because I create and express from my being. I am Love so all my actions are Love.

We are Love as we enter into this physical form. We are Love creating our own theatre of life as a human being. Our minds and our hearts get confused as we grow. We forget that we are Love and think we are only our bodies and our minds. We forget we are creators with The Universe, being Love.

I grew up going to church. I liked the energy, and I knew there was more than what appeared in front of my eyes. I always sensed the awe in nature. When I witnessed a dead person, I knew that some part of them was no longer present in their body. Their spirit, their consciousness had left; the energy that animated them was gone. The sacred animation of all of life is the mysterious presence of being alive. Knowing myself as this has allowed me to expand my curiosity, my creativity, and my love for all. There is more to us than meets the eye and that part holds many wonders.

Allowing The Mystery, ah the rub, I have been like a field lying fallow since retiring, waiting for the next calling. The transition time, much longer as it often is, has been a period of deep alchemical change happening below ground. This period has allowed me to fully step into loving myself, all others, and what is occurring around me. I have been polishing my diamantine self. I sense a call and yet The Mystery has not chosen to reveal it to me. I sit with this in meditation, trusting and being love, allowing magnetism to bring the next present. Equally, I can flip polarities and fear I am not doing as I should be. I feel I should be reaching striving as dictated by my old ways. Knowing myself has allowed my impatience a place at the table, a new approach. Trusting life has allowed Love to blossom more and more. I abide patiently, letting Love enter to bring a new way of being into my world. Always trusting.

We all walk in both the new and the old during these precious times of transition.

I have learnt more and more to listen deeply within to know myself and accept life as The Mystery it is. This attitude keeps my system relaxed; it allows ease and grace to flow in my life. May we trust change, knowing we are the change. Love can change the world.

May we each know ourselves as Love always.

Hypnosis

"For it is in your power to retire into yourself whenever you chose." *Marcus Aurelius*

I first experienced hypnosis to remove confusion as to what it is like and fear that I would not be in control and something bad would happen. It was a guided journey similar to a shamanic journey on the drum. It was relaxing and refreshing. Later during an energy medicine course, we used hypnosis to heal trauma from this life and past lives. This is called regression and it led me to tremendous healing. I use and enjoy light interactive hypnosis because I feel like I am fully present, yet I have somehow stepped to the side to allow communication with a wider and deeper part of my being. It is always relaxing and informative for me. The following is a session I had with a friend guiding me and recording anything I spoke during the experience. For me, the written recording of the experience and the discussion after with my friend helps me to recall all that occurred and secures it in my being.

I made my self comfortable, took a few deep breathes and dropped into my center. She asked me how I want to feel at the end of this session. I said, "Light, connected, and more knowing". She asked when I have felt light. My response was on the beach watching the moonrise, sailing, skiing. She chose sailing and we honed in on how I felt on the water while sailing. I described feeling free, connected to all the elements, blown clear and clean, and my aura scrubbed. Then we started the induction to the beach via stairs going down. I saw the beach briefly then sensed myself in a place of pink and yellow light with angels. She guided me down a path that felt like a cloudy swirl with doors. I came to a heavy wooden door with a rounded top and a crystal handle; the door swung inward. I stepped through and found myself on an earthen path, surrounded by a beautiful green forest. Then someone approached me from afar; this being came to me with deep love and honour, there was a beautiful heart connection. This being caressed my face gently, as a mother would do to a child, and encouraged me. This messenger told me, "You can do it" and "You are the Light so be the Light". The depth of love and tenderness brought tears to my eyes. Then this being merged energetically into my solar plexus, I felt the energy mix with my light and it went super bright. I felt this was a soul retrieval returning tenderness and love for myself to me. Every cell in my body was tingling and felt super alive, it was a cellular healing. Suddenly an image of a dragonfly appeared. I felt the energy shifting, opening my chakras especially in my back. I felt like everything was being tuned like a radio.

Then I felt like I was on a cloud with other beings looking down on to Earth. We were making plans. I felt so much love for the planet and her people. There was love, joy of doing, being who we are, and all was aligned. Then I began having sensations inside in my lower belly, I realized I was birthing something although it was very gentle. I was birthing peace all over the globe. The energy I birthed seem to swirl out around the globe like a mist. I had a sense of it penetrating everything. Peace was being created. The energy of peace wrapped around the planet and infiltrated everything with swirls and wisps. It went deep into some places, it swirled around people and they awoke startled that they ever acted in any other way than peace. They totally accepted that peace is who they are. The mist seemed to be violet with pink then rainbows of colour, it was beautiful to behold.

Suddenly everything went white. I knew that the mist was still happening on earth. I simply needed to allow it and let it go on. I remember thinking like raising children. My heart energy began pulsing. Then pink light came up my body and into my head. I felt a sense of infinite joy and there was a density to it, a solidness. There was a depth of knowing that "All is well". Then I felt a known pain that quickly dissolved. I began to feel tingling in my feet and was told, "You are receiving the peace that earth was receiving". An explanation came that they were making it linear and separate for me so I could see and understand it yet truly it was all happening at once. Then I had loads of sensations in my body that were dissolving anything that is not peace.

During the next scene, I was sitting on a throne, being crowned. I felt the orb and spectre being placed in my hands and the robes on my shoulders. They were gorgeous visually and sensation wise. The robes were deep purple with white ermine fur trim. All of this seemed to anchor into my chakras from bottom to top. Finally lighting up the crown, I was wearing, with energy. It was all very gentle. I heard, "We understand child, it is the way it had to be". I felt this summed up my childhood experiences which caused me to close myself down and dim my light. Then I felt dominos flipping over or little doors opening around my heart, like a Rolodex flipping open, it was working my heart free. Then a soft orange and yellow light like gentle fire came into my solar plexus and moved up into my neck. My head began moving slowly and sounds emerged from within me and progressed into light language. This carried on for a bit and then I felt a lot of energy around my face and saw white light everywhere. I found myself flying on the back of a huge eagle. I was connecting back to the beach, our starting point. I was told, "You are the sun". Then I arrived at the beach, covered myself with sand, and focused on the sounds and sensations to be there. My intentions were fulfilled I felt like pure light, totally connected and I had been given much knowing. I absorbed all that happened and brought it into my physical depths as I returned to ordinary reality. It is so exciting and so cool. Birthing peace was incredible! Knowing that it is here now even more so! It makes me want to sing with joy!

Trusting the multitude of healing modalities that exist in our world is important. Trusting that you know what is best for you is essential. We must always be discerning when we make choices to follow any path. I offer this look at hypnosis simply as an example and an experience which brought me expanded love and awareness.

May we all find our unique way to heal.

Peace

*"Until he extends his circle of compassion to include all
living things, man will not himself find peace."*
Albert Schweitzer

Peace that passeth all understanding. An attempt to explain the unexplainable, and yet still I strive. For me, peace is a felt sense within. It is palpable in the air when it has been allowed. It is a wide-open space of potential and connection that holds so much vibrancy and aliveness. It contains an unveiling of truth that we are all the same, and underneath all our humanness the pulse is peaceful acceptance of everything. It is a sacred quality that penetrates and disperses all complex human nature and allows the divine to enter. It arises spontaneously and creates awe when it is present. It is a vibrant power of stillness revealed.

I came to my contemplative life desiring peace within. My life was a normal busy time of growing responsibilities and I needed solace. I would sit on my pillow or lie down, allowing myself to sink into a deep place inside that connected me to a slower pace and feeling of connection. I felt this is who I am. I learnt to calm the outer chatter and persistent nagging by acceptance and gently turning toward the calm. An image I use is of sinking deep into the ocean to the place of stillness and peace. During SCUBA years ago, I had come to know this sensation of the ocean depth. The light at depth has a soothing, gentle quality of mystery and peace for me. The contrast being the turbulence at the surface. The disturbances of the wind, the waves, the cross currents, and eddies can create anxiety and fear. When you sink into the depth of the ocean peace is present, things move with grace, and the interconnection of life is felt. Peace in the depth of the ocean has served me well as a touchstone image for returning to my calm center, breathing, and regrouping to move forward. When I let myself sink away from the surface tensions and anxieties that create turbulence in my life, a window can open where I thought a door had closed. I can navigate choices and actions with clarity, kindness, and acceptance. I can choose calming solutions and nurture myself with love as I courageously move forward in life.

Becoming peaceful about energies and emotions that I experience in my body has relaxed my nervous system. I sometimes feel jumpy energy that is far from peaceful as it makes my whole system agitated. Once I realized that this energy was excitement, I could calmly allow it space.

I am allowed to be excited and full of energy; this is who I am, there is nothing to fear. I am no longer a child; I can allow this energy to be present and real for the highest good of all. I do not need to contain this energy to meet the suffering of others. I do not need to bring myself down to their energetic level to belong. This is me and this is how I am here and now. I am a highly energetic, loving, clear, and embodied divine human being. This is who I am. I am grateful that my journey has allowed me to become peaceful with energies that move in my system.

It is an important lesson to be aware that fear and excitement are on the same continuum. I am a very kinaesthetic person, I feel. I feel even more when I touch you. I am an empath and can easily take on your energy. This does not serve you or me. I am learning to accept the energy of excitement as wonderful. I am realizing that excitement and fear can feel the same: butterflies inside. Truly, I guess it is part of learning to be with both, slowing down, breathing, and allowing them each their own expression. Loving what is present, giving what is present space to be as it will be, and trusting that everything is always in constant motion and changing. Everything cycles, it comes and goes. The excitement will arise, and then it will return from where it came. Fear will do the same if we allow it the space to do so. Much like the waves coming in and out on the shore in their own way. Waves can be gentle or crashing. Either way, they are part of the beautiful ocean touching the sacred land.

I have led my life with the attitude and attention to create peaceful times. If I am embarking on an activity that is challenging my abilities, I will use visualization to help me stay calm. I will hum a tune or find myself counting in my head to keep the pressure of my overactive mind at bay. I will breathe deeply and consciously release tension in my muscles. All of this is to create a space for peace within a challenge.

Being peaceful is a choice. It a choice we can make even if life is full and busy. We can move through whatever is presenting in a peaceful accepting manner, or we can wind ourselves up into a stressed-out non-stop whirlwind. May we all know we are the ocean and the wave. May we all learn to be peace even in the turbulence of life.

May peace find its way into all our lives, all our actions, and all our relationships. Peace is revealed once we release tensions, concerns, and preconceived notions. Peace is a presence and truth.

May we all cultivate our lives so peace flourishes.

Part 4 - Creativity

Creativity is a birthright as a human being. We are creative problem-solving beings. Spend a few minutes watching a toddler figure out how to get something it wants and you will see ingenuity at it best. Sadly, as we grow in this world, we often close down our creative nature. We impose limitations on the quality of whatever we create. It needs to look realistic, it has to rhyme, it has to match, it has to please another's ear, or it has to have a purpose. The list goes on and on until we are immobilized and no longer dare consider that we can do anything creative. Then we limit ourselves because we only consider creativity a piece of art, a poem or music. We forget that a beautifully laid table for dinner is creative. The decorating of a cake, the application of makeup, the choice of clothing, designing anything, the arranging or planting of flowers, cooking, and even cleaning are all creative acts. So much depends on our outlook and willingness to see creativity in our lives. When nothing feels creative, finding small baby step ways to introduce a small change that appeals and brings a moment of joy is a beginning. Listening to a new song, stopping and swaying along to the music can lead to full-on kitchen dancing. Walking a new route can introduce a fresh outlook. I was a creative child, always making things or making up words or poems. Over time I limited myself to staying within the lines and keeping my creations to myself. I continued to create, it simply lacked imagination and boundless expression. I exchanged macaroni mobiles for sewing patterns. I exchanged free drawings for colouring books. I eventually stopped singing, stopped writing poetry, stopped drawing and stayed firmly within the recipes while cooking. Fortunately, my children allowed me to dabble alongside them as they experimented with their creativity. Thus, I managed to keep a current of creativity alive in myself.

At one point, I had a dream that I was dragging around a frozen body that was face down, hidden from me. It was attached to me by a rope and I felt like I was going around in circles with it dragging along a rather barren terrain. That morning I explored where I felt frozen energy within myself, when it started and how it was holding me back. I discovered with deep love and understanding that it became frozen to create safety for me. It was clear to me that I froze my natural creativity and expression in the world so that I could monitor the world around me on high level alert to keep myself safe. I did a journey with the intention to allow the frozen self to transmute. It thawed into liquid water that flowed everywhere in my system carrying creativity into all aspects of my life. I learned how my natural creative self desires to continually express. The healing moved me to make creative expression a priority in my life. I am here, as everyone is, being a unique creative experience in the cosmic tapestry of life.

How we each express our creativity is as diverse and unique as we each are in our appearance. So many of us get caught up thinking that what they make needs to be perfect. Tendencies to judge ourselves and insist on perfection often limit our willingness to leap into a new adventure. A creative act does not need to be grandiose. It is often the simplest acts of creativity such as wearing a new colour, cooking a new recipe, or singing a nonsensical song that can bring joy into our system. The joy and excitement encourage us to keep trying things that are fresh and new. I have many ways of expressing my creative nature. Some are just for me and make me smile and laugh inside myself. Other creations are visible to share with others. I am presenting a few that bring me joy regularly.

May we all know ourselves as creators and be filled with courage to express our talents.

Acrostics

"The true sign of intelligence is not knowledge but imagination." Albert Einstein

An acrostic is a phrase formed using the letters of another word. It can also be a poem created by using each letter of a word. I use this as a creative tool to shift limiting beliefs around words. A common example is FEAR stands for False Expectations Appearing Real.

This creative technique has been a form of healing play for me for years. It started with the word God. I come from a Christian based background and the old man in white robes in the sky image was dominate whenever I thought about the word God. I never bought into the wrathful we are sinners' story. I did have a sense that I had to do what God said or something might bad might happen. This added to my people pleasing behaviour. As my metaphysical life expanded, I needed to shift these beliefs and befriend the creator energy as a part of me. This led to the acrostic Grace of Divinity for God. Now when I hear the word God, I feel the flow of grace aligning in my system. I know and feel that I am part of God as Grace of Divinity. The old belief system no longer has an emotional charge in my system. I feel connected to all the grace of life.

The power of words is important to acknowledge and feel. Becoming aware of the words we use and the energy behind them allows us to be more precise and authentic in our communication. Understanding that our words are vibratory energy moving outward into the collective field helps us to clean up our language. Monitoring our casual use of words, whether positive or negative, is voicing our opinion with respect. When I speak, I want to show respect and honour for myself and the one I am addressing. I choose to contribute to the energy of this world and beyond with kindness, consideration, and love, including my words.

The word love has been another area of difficulty for me in the past. Love carried images of romantic fairy tales, being swept away by love and a multitude of other culturally conditioned images. My way to remove these limiting beliefs was to use the acrostic Light of Vitality Everywhere for Love. This made love into light energy for me. Light that is critical for life, exists everywhere, and can travel anywhere. Light like the sun which beams its energy forth with generous abundance, available to everyone equally. Now when I say "I love you" I know and feel that I am sending you energy to support life. The sticky old cultural energy has dissolved and is no longer mucking up the intention. I send Love as Light of Vitality Everywhere to many people and situations throughout the day. It is clean and clear as love and light are one and the same for me.

I have listed a few other acrostics that have supported my growth and helped me to˙ dispel old limiting belief patterns. The essential idea is to take away the spell that the word has had over your life and replace it with fresh ideas to be considered. It allows a mini contemplation of words that can create significant changes in your reaction to hearing those words spoken. It is a magical and fun practice that I have enjoyed for years.

HEALING - Hold Energy Align Light Inspire Natural Grace

SHAME - Self Hatred About My Experience

TRUST - Truly Rely Upon Spirit Teaching

LIFE - Love In Full Expression

UNCERTAINTY - Underneath Nerves, Creative Energy, Really Trust And It Naturally Teaches You

SOUL - Supra Optimized Unique Light

HOPE - Heaven On Planet Earth

BEING - Beautiful Energy In Natural Grace

BEING - Beaming Energy Into Now Gently

FAITH - Feeling Always Interconnected Totally Holistic

PEACE - Personal Energy Allowing Creative Expression

Acrostics are a playful way to shift the energy around words and what we have come to believe about those words. It is a creative, fun way to enjoy removing energy charges from words. I often come up with one version that is perfect at that moment and later I change it entirely. There is nothing set in stone. I write them down so I can see them and read them aloud which allows my brain to shift from the old belief pathway to a new one. It is playful which means one day it may occur one way and another day it is something new. I allow acrostics be fun.

May imagination and creativity shift the power of words in our systems.

Painting

*"Every child is an artist. The problem is how to remain
an artist once he grows up."* Pablo Picasso

My journey with painting and art has been
convoluted and rather full of self-deprecation. I
loved art in school. Yet my creations rarely passed my
own judgement when I looked around at others' abilities
and talents. Comparison is a definitive killer of creativity.
I finally took myself off to art classes to learn to draw
when I was in my late forties. It was quite miraculous.
When I was given some instruction, the task became
enjoyable, and the outcomes were quite acceptable. I was
encouraged to move into painting and managed that as
well. I have always loved colour so the blending and
discovery of new shades was exciting. I now have my own
artwork decorating my home.

Going through this journey from criticism and doubt to
acceptance and joy has been part of my own healing. I had

done enough work, loving and accepting myself as I am, to step into the possibility of putting paint to canvas. I continued to feel the fear of failure and being unworthy as I showed up with my art supplies. It was daunting and my mantra was simply you can always start again. Fortunately, I had the support of a good teacher who firmly believed everyone has an artist inside them. I continued to love myself no matter the outcome and deepened my own foundation of trust, love, and learning not to care what anyone else thought of my creation. I learnt never to take another's comment personally as it is always from their lenses of expectation and experience. I gave myself time to develop abilities without any pressure of have to, should do, or ought to. I eventually moved into a greater intuitive place of flow with my artistic creations.

I began with copying photos and learning techniques, giving myself room to develop. I started small with creating abstract backgrounds of multiple colours, then a totem animal would call to be painted. I moved to larger canvases of abstract colours and designs. Throughout, my confidence has been built up. Equally, I still sit in front of a canvas wondering what am I doing. Fortunately, I have learnt to trust the process, stay with the process, and stay out of my own way as Kathy Altman[ix] taught in dance workshops. I still cringe when someone calls me an artist and truth be told I am a multidimensional creative with many talents. Being an artist is one of them. More and more I accept my way of creating is through my intuitive flow and am always excited about the outcome.

I now paint when called. I get an intuitive notion to buy a canvas, often months ahead, and it sits. I wonder and carry on with my life. Out of the blue, I find myself thinking about what wants to be painted, colours, and textures. Then, while I am out walking, I find myself contemplating the painting that wants to come forth. So, it begins, I set up with my supplies, good music, and trust. I simply start and am always amazed at the end by the art which emerges.

I have created sculptures using chandler crystals and painted canvases. I have finger painted, then applied stickers in geometric forms to the plexiglass. I have done fluid paintings. I am willing to try things and play. I accept failures and carry on. It is truly an outlet of play and experimentation. I receive beautiful messages of hope and encouragement from the creations. I allow myself to dream beyond my limitations to imagine possibilities and bring forth that which is calling to become. Creating is pure joy for me.

May we all take risks to create beyond our imagination and have fun doing so.

Music

"Music is a moral law. It gives soul to the universe, wings to the mind, flight to the imagination and charm and gaiety to life and to everything." Plato

I sing to bring high vibration energy into my system and to allow it to move in the universe as it will. When I sing, I feel the peace, the love, and the joy of being alive as palpable energy that surrounds me. I am bringing forth love.

When I sing, I simply center my being, take a breath or two, open my mouth, and the notes flow out on my voice. There are no words to occupy the brain, only melodic tones come forth. My eyes are closed this seems to increase the focalization of the energy and there is less distraction. The more relaxed I am and comfortable in my environment, trusting those I am with, the easier it is. The energy that emanates seems to apply to the moment as a form of healing. This is my form of channelling which is simply bringing forth energy from a higher dimension into the reality I find myself.

I have always loved to sing. As a young girl, I played the piano in the basement and sung at the top of my lungs. I remember enjoying elementary school concerts and singing fun songs like "Tea for two and two for tea". I would simply have said singing made me happy. It still does. I often discover myself humming a tune as I work in the kitchen or recalling snippets of a tune or lyrics that make me smile.

I enjoy listening to music it has a calming effect for my body. It can keep my heart open when more chaotic energy is happening around me. Headphones and iPods allowed me to remain focused and at ease while my teenage boys were playing video games with repetitive mind-numbing themes. Listening to peaceful tunes helps me navigate any frenetic energy like a busy airport.

Many of us have difficulty allowing our voices to be heard. I am no different, having been told, "You are tone-deaf and cannot carry a tune". I have been self-conscious of my singing for years. I finally took a few singing lessons when I was in my early forties. This freed me up to be happier, singing happy birthday aloud. I continue to feel awkward about my singing of songs. I have a terrible time remembering words to a song. Perhaps I was never to get caught up in the expression of song words so that I can bring in divine notes. So that the purity of energy could flow without being impeded by my human construct around words and tunes. When the musical notes flow through my voice it brings in a high, clear level of peace and love energy. Each time it is new and fresh for the moment I find myself.

My first experience with divine singing occurred when I was having a reiki session. I was feeling lots of jumbled emotions in my body. The practitioner said, "If any sounds or singing arise allow them out". Then it began deep tones from my heart expressing the grief held within it, my whole body was vibrating. What came forth was moving the energy in my being I could feel the releases and shifts in my body. Then an angelic-like tone came forth and emitted such beauty, peace, and love that healed my being and held in the surrounding space. Later I dreamt of a woman within me and she was singing the most beautiful melody. The words repeated, "You are love". It filled me with such love for myself and life. Thus, the journey began which moved me to take a few singing lessons to help myself have more ease with my voice.

My physiotherapy career did not lend itself to breaking into song, and the life pace of teenagers halted further emergence of singing. While attending an energy medicine course, the divine notes emerged once again starting with whistling high-pitched sounds that were somehow assisting the healing being done. Then light language began with a fierce energy that would penetrate the physical and those willing to receive it, healing as it vibrated. I received these vibrations into my physical and energetic being with much shifting, opening, and changes being felt along with great comfort and support. Light language is nonsensical words that are channelled from spirit. The energy pours forth and is emitted and received without activating the brain which would try to analyze any words. I was blessed to learn of Judy Satori[x] who spoke and called it light language and offered information via the internet. This allowed me to understand that what I was experiencing was a reality for others and is a possibility for anyone.

I continue to use light language for personal healing. I sing to the ocean when I am at the beach. I sing love songs to the water. I speak light language and sing to friends; these are blessings of love for them. I have allowed myself to speak light language and to sing in groups. I have been encouraged to move from speaking to singing. The singing is a higher, clearer love vibration that passes through me into the world. I welcome the gift to be able to express this love energy to the world. I delight in the creative healing energy that comes through these divine notes.

May we each trust our voice to bring beauty to our world.

Dance

"O body swayed to music, O brightening glance,
How can we know the dancer from the dance?"
William Butler Yeats

When I was six, I began figure skating. It was a slow start as I could not do cross cuts in the hand me down skates with collapsed ankles. When I was nine, I got my very own new skates. I took off from there. I loved being at the rink whizzing around on the ice, spending time doing figure of eights and feeling free. I continued figure skating through high school, loving the movement, the music, and the fantasy of being grace in motion. The Spring before I headed to university in Halifax their ice rink burnt down. Thus, ended my figure skating days because there were no facilities when I arrived at university.

Gratefully, years later I discover *5Rhythms®* dance which was developed by Gabrielle Roth[xi]. The weekly sessions I

139

first attended were called "*Sweat Your Prayers*". This free form of dance, in a cyclical wave of flow, staccato, chaos, lyrical, and stillness, returned me to the freedom of the ice rink. The music spoke to my soul and the ability to move as my body desired was blissful. I had found my creative expression through movement once again. Dance gave me a place to express anything and everything. I would dance frustration about my kids, grief around loss, boredom from routine and joy of being alive and moving. I explored all my emotional states on the dance floor being with whatever arose in the moment and allowing it to move me. I did workshops that stretched my comfort zones. They offered a safe container for trial and error always with movement, music, and change. I continue to participate in conscious dance. It is a place for me to bring my prayers into motion, to align with all that I am, and to feel connected to everything beyond time and space. It is a moving meditation that fills me with joy and aliveness. It is a place where my inner figure skater gets to jump, whirl, and twirl to great tunes and be grace in motion.

Movement is essential to my being. I am most grounded and feel my best in motion. I am an avid walker, love my treadmill for running, ride my bicycle, practise Tai Chi, and dance around my kitchen. The balance of motion and stillness throughout my day seems to align my being to the greater whole. The coalescing of the motion and the stillness that happens is a sweet spot of purity, freedom, and alignment. It is a point of conscious connection with The Mystery and knowing I am that. The athletic world would call it being in the zone. It is being in the flow of life with love. It is magnificent. It is available to all of us as we move in whatever way brings us pleasure.

I feel a great connection watching motion. The ease and grace of an animal running or a human performing dance or sport, these invoke the perfection that we are dynamic vessels of motion. The marvel of the breath moving in and out of our body is motion even in the most still states of meditation. The resilience and the grace of the human body has always fascinated me. The outer motion of limbs created by timing of joint motion, balance and reflexes. The inner motion of cellular activity dancing in response to our biology. It is all the beauty of living in motion, glorious and alive.

May we all dance our unique dance knowing ourselves as divine human beings.

Writing

"The mystical life is at the centre of all that I do and all that I think and all that I write." William Butler Yeats

Free writing, stream of consciousness writing, the movement of the pen across the page, letting words arise into form. I take up a pen and allow the words to flow as a daily practice. This is a practice I have committed to for the past few years. It has brought forth healing, fun, and more love for myself and our human condition. I have resisted this practice for years. I felt I did not have the time. I had no idea what I would write. I held back. I had read *The Artist's Way* by Julia Cameron[xii] years before. I tried the exercise twice and life took over. Her practice is called *"Morning Pages"*. Upon waking, you write three pages of continuous writing, freehand. This is not to read and ruminate. It is a method to get information out of your head on to the page. Doing so allows the mind and emotions to rest into the Now and move in life with greater clarity and ease. It can certainly evoke lots of emotions. My experience is that moving the thoughts swirling in my mind and body to the paper makes room to find solace and peace. In my way, I have used this free writing at various times of day, I have stopped and journeyed into my inner space to move energies. I have laughed and I have cried as I navigate my life written right in front of me. It continues to be a healing tool that helps me be peace and love.

I remember writing poetry as a child and in my teens. I have always loved writing letters. It is a form of expression that is private and shared with trusted companions. The pace of writing has always suited me. I can linger and ponder what it is that I which to express to another. I can wait, then send a letter or email after I have slept on my response. This is important to remember in our fast-paced world of texting and email. There is often good reason to not push the send button immediately. A good night's sleep can bring to light new revelations that would have been missed, or can allow space to consider the energetics behind the words that have been written. All words spoken and written carry energy forth into the collective field. It is wise to always consider what you are contributing to the whole. My preference is attention, accuracy, and love when I am communicating. May we all communicate for the highest good of all.

It is through the morning pages that this book came forth to be written through me. An adventure for my humanness and my divine self. I have had hints that I would write a book one day for years. I have never taken it that seriously as I simply had no idea what to write and life had a knack of keeping me busy. Then the idea called to write to my unborn grandchildren. I sat with this idea and began writing some essays. I received encouragement from a writer I met while out walking, to continue, and another burst of writing happened. I kept getting the push to write and yet I felt immobilized. My inner critic was doing a fabulous job of reining me into a defeatist attitude. As happens, the universe stepped in and brought forth information for me to approach from a different angle. I began doing shamanic journeywork that brought me in touch with a supportive guide for the book and my inner muse showed up. She is a powerful creative energy that is filled with joy. I moved into my heart space around the book to approach from love instead of what-ifs and fear. I sat upon my comfy red chair in my inner heart cave, bringing love to the process and all my holdbacks. One day a hole in the ground opened beside my chair. It had a ladder. I climbed down and discovered a brilliant light emitting and realized it was the book. I brought it up from the depths to my chair where I placed it and left it. Then I began using my daily walks and my morning pages to contemplate the book and what it wanted to bring forth. Essentially, I began to love the book instead of criticizing the writing, beating myself up about how long it was taking for me to write, and the multiple unknowns that were swirling me into avoidance. I made the choice to stop limiting myself. I moved forward with writing from my higher self and accepted that there is value to this book. I then began feeling like the book was in my hands and could visualize it present with its own wings. I have had encouragement from spirit to continue and complete the book. I have had reminders that it is a vibrational gift of love that has healed much for me and offers the same to others who are waiting to read it. I have increased my commitment to producing the book. I have aligned with the joy that the book desires to bring forth to forge ahead with the writing. The life of this book is ongoing. The writing is close to complete. The remainder of the journey is a vast unknown that I am trusting will unfold in its own time and course. I have held this book as my baby and once it is launched into the world it will have its own flight path which is truly none of my business. I am grateful for all the healing, ruminating, discussions, and contemplations it has provided me. This book is its own presence emerging.

May it bring joy, love, and peace to all who read it.

Raising Children with Love

*"Life affords no greater responsibility, no greater
privilege, than the raising of the next generation."*
C. Everett Koop

I remember wondering whether I would be loving when
I was pregnant. I truly did not know that the moment
one of these little beings arrived in my arms that I would
experience love beyond any description. I did, the
miracle, the preciousness, and the innocence set off a
cascade of love instantly. When my second son arrived, I
wondered if I could love another one as much as the first.
Once again love took hold and expanded making room in
my heart for each one. Love is an endless, eternal flame
of joy that my wee ones sparked in me with ease. When
one of my children enters the room or sends a text, I feel
myself brighten up. I feel my eyes sparkle and dance with
the joy of sharing life with these unique beings. I feel our

unity beyond our human selves. My soul dances in delight.

Raising children has been a gift of creativity and love in my life. I was once asked by an older gentleman, "What I had done to have such great kids?". My answer was immediate and simple: "I loved them". It even surprised me as I could have denied my role. I could have listed the numerous reasons they were not great, especially as they were in their teen years. Instead, I chose to accept that my love was a good influence on my kids and that they are great just as they are. I remind myself of this in moments that appear less great in my mind.

Do not get me wrong, raising children is a lifetime commitment of love, acceptance, and patience. It is hard work without any manual. When our third child arrived, I realized I only had two hands. I could have used dozens. She was born in October before the annual time change. My boys were early risers, I am not. I remember waking to everyone being up and ready for the day at 4:45 am. I was shocked. The day ahead seemed endless. I did create an easy system for the boys to get their breakfast. I would lie in bed half sleeping, half listening for a disaster to ensue. We survived that and many more ups and downs of life with children.

For me, parenting has been a continual shattering of beliefs and shifting of focus. I used routines and early bed to survive the early years. I did years of solo parenting as my husband was in the Navy. Organization and friends were magic. I did make space for my own life in those years. I mastered my knitting machines, I learnt Tai Chi and I worked at my clinic to keep my sanity. Life was full and rapid fire. I dropped into bed exhausted regularly. It was life happening full on. I would not change a thing today.

I am always amazed at the extremes in life. I love my kids deeply no question and they could make me furious. I have been stunned by how angry my children could make me. This is a planet of duality in action and paradoxical. I remember getting myself outside on the deck to have a deep breath and count to ten on several occasions as I was wrangling life with three bright inquiring minds. I am grateful to acknowledge that nowadays the flares of anger have turned into flames of passion for life and loving myself through everything that arises. Deeply acknowledging that the anger was truly fear that I was not up to the job of child raising, fearing that I would be blamed for all outcomes. When I realized how this fear could paralyze me, I began learning to trust myself, life, and everyone's journey.

In my parenting history, I certainly did things that I am not proud of. My daughter is quick to remind me of the wooden spoon that I broke on the kitchen counter trying to stop some dispute. I once poured apple sauce over my eldest's head in sheer frustration of his not wanting to eat.

I threatened, cajoled, and pleaded with them to stop arguing. None of it pretty. All of it life with kids.

I started my meditation practise when they were young. It saved me. I learnt to see a bigger picture. I learnt to forgive my shortcomings and outbursts. I learnt to accept myself. I learnt to accept that they are their own light being selves doing life. A calm descended within me and the rocky road days smoothed out by applying love for myself and them.

My eldest took most of the brunt of my learning curve in parenting. Pretty normal. When he was in his twenties, I apologized for my behaviours. He was open to hearing my confessions and forgiving me my conduct. He did not remember each detail but I opened up fully, it was healing and our relationship has more love. This idea of returning to my errors and apologizing to my kids came from reading a friend's thesis on her experience doing something similar. It is a valuable consideration which created healing paths for me.

Today, my children are young adults making their way in the world. They know how to love and care for themselves. They know how to be kind and considerate as they move in the world. They share their lives with us and we are happy to join in the fun.

Loving these human beings has been a joy for me. I still love to see them arrive home and love to see them go.

They have their lives to expand and grow and so do I. We can share our journeys of ups and downs with strong relationships. I am grateful.

May all children be loved and adored for the precious beings they are.

Closing Words

I am a flower of love that has blossomed and is allowing her essence to float on the wind for others to pick up and enjoy as they will. All love always!

This book is planting seeds of unity consciousness among readers. It contains essences of truth throughout. It is a pointing towards, an indicator of openings and possibilities for consideration and contemplation. It is my prayer that all can gain a small piece of wisdom that can help them build a more loving, beauty-filled life. A life that honours both our divinity and our humanness as our whole loving self. A life that allows love to lead the way, peace to descend within, and joy to erupt in every cell. A life that knows their light is vital to the world. A life that shines bright for others to see. A life that flows with the wholeness of love in action. A life of love, peace, and joy.

Loving ourselves as we are is a giant first step. It takes accepting baby steps to walk the path of love. It takes falling down, getting up, brushing yourself off, and carrying on over and over. My spirit guides would say, "Keep on keeping on". May you be blessed with the courage to trust the process and keep on keeping on. Allowing my soul into the driver's seat of my life has allowed me to soar on wings of love. This is my wish for you, dear precious reader.

Acknowledgments

I have completed this book with the support of friends, family and newcomers to my life. I am deeply grateful to my friends, Deborah Hartford, Jayne Harvey, Cindi Kereszti, Ana-La-Rai Sagle, and Mary Wilkie for listening as I sorted out ideas, wording, hopes, and fears. Everyone needs a team of cheerleaders rallying for them.

I am deeply appreciative and grateful to Corinne Aarsen (CorinneAarsenBooks.com) for her expertise about editing, book design and publishing. Deep bow to Sherry Ridout, Darinka Popovic, Jaz Snider, and Stewart Keenan for reading, editing and keeping me going to the finish line with their support.

Thank You

About the Author

Anne Round is a retired physiotherapist who lives in Victoria, British Columbia, Canada. She is dedicated to maintaining a healthy body, mind and spirit. She is a voyager who brings her light everywhere she shows up.

Recommended Reading List

I have complied a small list of authors and teachers whose works have assisted me with my blossoming. They all have wonderful books. They can be found on social media with videos and newsletters. Further references from the text can be seen in the End Notes.

Richard Rudd, Gene Keys <u>genekeys.com</u>

Bruce Lipton, Biology of Belief <u>www.brucelipton.com</u>

Brené Brown, Gifts of Imperfection <u>brenebrown.com</u>

Liz Gilbert, Big Magic <u>www.elizabethgilbert.com</u>

End Notes

i Gregg Braden www.greggbraden.com

ii Masaru Emoto www.masaru-emoto.net/en

iii Kathy Altman openfloor.org

iv Danielle Laporte www.daniellelaporte.com

v HeartMath Institute www.heartmath.com

vi Sharon Leslie sharonleslie.com

vii Matt Kahn mattkahn.org

viii Richard Rudd, *The Art of Contemplation.* 2018 Genekeys.com

ix Kathy Altman openfloor.org

x Judy Satori judysatori.com

xi Gabrielle Roth *5Rhythms®* www.5rhythms.com

xii Cameron, Julia, *The Artist's Way.* TarcherPerigee, 1992 juliacameronlive.com